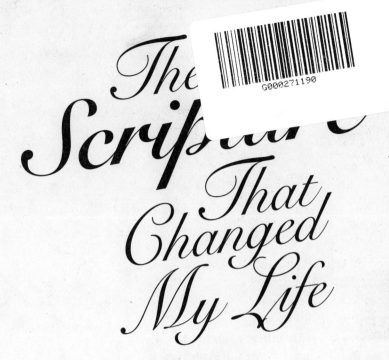

The Scripture That Changed My Life

**True stories of
people whose
lives were
changed by
a single Bible
passage**

Ron and Dorothy Watts

Pacific Press® Publishing Association
Nampa, Idaho
Oshawa, Ontario, Canada

Edited by Glen Robinson
Designed by Tim Larson

Copyright © 1999 by
Pacific Press® Publishing Association
Printed in the United States of America
All Rights Reserved

Watts, Ron, 1936–
    The scripture that changed my life : true stories of people whose
lives were changed by a single Bible passage / Ron and Dorothy
Watts.
        p.   cm.
    Includes bibliographical references and index.
    ISBN 0-8163-1583-3
    1. Christian biography. 2. Bible—Influence. I. Watts, Dorothy
Eaton., 1937– . II. Title.
BR1702.W355 1999
270'.092'2—dc21
[B]   97-43214
                                                              CIP

99 00 01 02 03 • 5 4 3 2 1

Table of Contents

Introduction

The great privilege of every believer is that as a priest each can go directly to God through His Word without the mediation of another human being. God manifests Himself to us in His Word. He will speak to us just as clearly as He spoke to Samuel and Isaiah.

Our privilege as priests

This is part of what Peter means when he says we are a special people, a royal priesthood. The priests not only presented the needs and confessions of the people to God, but they heard God speaking to them messages for the people.

As priests, we have the privilege of going directly to God and hearing Him speak directly to us through His Word. Through His Word, God can speak to us just as clearly today as He did to prophets and priests long ago.

Encounters with God in Scripture

The forty stories in this book are all true stories of men and women who found strength through a single passage of Scripture during a time of personal crisis. Here are the stories of people who faced death, bankruptcy, uncontrollable fear, kidnapping, cancer, poverty, homelessness, addiction, and imprisonment. These are stories of people who found that God's Word gave them hope in times of mental illness, martyrdom, shipwreck, fires, business difficulties, career change, and ravaging disease.

The forty people whose experiences are related sensed God speaking directly to them as they opened His Word. They knew He was near and real and able to do what He had promised. There was life-giving, energizing, overcoming power for them in their encounter with God in Scripture.

Leapfrogging the generations

It would have been such a privilege to have been born 2,000 years ago, so that we might talk with Jesus as Peter, James, and John did. Or at least we might have talked with those who met Him face to face.

However, that is exactly what we can do, now, by opening the Bible and meditating on its pages. We can leapfrog the generations in our spiritual experience.

1 John 1:1-3 teaches this amazing truth.

That which was from the beginning, which we have heard, which we have seen with our eyes, which we have looked upon, and our hands have handled, of the Word of life (For the life was manifested, and we have seen it, and bear witness, and shew unto you that eternal life, which was with the Father, and was manifested unto us;); That which we have seen and heard declare we unto you, that ye also may have fellowship with us: and truly our fellowship is with the Father, and with his Son Jesus Christ.

The apostles and prophets who wrote the Scriptures had a first-hand experience of the presence of God. When we in a deliberate and meaningful way read, study, and meditate on Scripture, we enter into that firsthand fellowship with God that they had. The writers of the Bible had personal contact directly with God. We, too, participate in their personal fellowship and contact with God when we read the record they left of that experience.

The stories in this book are proof that Christian experience does not need to come to us a hundred generations later through the tradition passed on to us through some kind of diluted apostolic succession. We can leapfrog the generations and directly communicate with divinity through direct participation with those who had the immediate experience and recorded it in Scripture.

Meeting the Author

"The Bible is the only book on planet earth where the Author is always present while it is being read," writes Evelyn Christianson. (Christianson, *What Happens When God Answers,* p. 46.)

We have been surprised at the enthusiasm people have had to meet us as the authors of *Powerful Passages.* They have stood in line to get our autographs and have gone out of their way to tell us how thrilled they were to meet us.

"Yet, the very God of the universe is present with us every time we read His book. But how few of us treat the Bible that way! How little awe or excitement we display at having its Author, the very God of heaven, actually speaking to us about our personal needs and desires" (Christianson, p. 460).

The forty people whose stories are told in this book were ones who recognized the very presence of the Author with them as they read.

*I am the Lord thy God which have brought thee out of
the land of Egypt out of the house of bondage.*

Touched at Her Bedside

In the early 1700s, Ebenezer Erskine was one of the most notable evangelical preachers among Presbyterians in Scotland. Crowds of thousands came to his parish church at Portmoak in Kinros to hear his powerful preaching. Years after his death in 1754 his sermons continued to be republished and widely read.

But this was not so in the early days of his ministry. For the first four years of his pastorate there seemed to be no fire in the altar of his heart.

The son of a minister, he studied in the University of Edinburgh and was awarded an M.A. degree. He was ordained and assigned the parish of Portmoak. But he began his ministry, he says, "without much zeal, callously and mechanically, being swallowed up in unbelief and in rebellion against God." He felt no enthusiasm for the Bible and found the New Testament boring. His sermons were long and formal, repeated parrotlike after he had memorized the scripts.

For four long years, his wife, Alison, wept in secret over her husband's unspirited ministry and unregenerate heart. Then she became seriously ill. Racked with fever, she raved deliriously. Her spiritual distress for her husband was a shock to his ears and caused him to search his heart.

He began to pray and plead with God for the healing of his wife. In answer to his prayers, she became calm and slept peacefully. Erskine wrote in his diary: "This I think was the first time that ever I felt the Lord touching my heart. . . . Her distress and her deliverance were blessed to me."

A few days later they were sitting in his study talking together of spiritual things. Suddenly a powerful text of scripture came to him in a new and living way. It was Exodus 20:2, the introduction to the Ten Commandments: "I am the Lord your God."

He remembered a time when he was ten years old and his minister father took him to a class for the children at Dryburgh Abbey. He recalled how his father read from the shorter catechism, "What is the preface to the Ten Commandments?"

Then he read the answer: "I am the Lord thy God which have brought thee out of the land of Egypt, out of the house of bondage." It had taken hold of young Ebenezer's mind when he was ten.

That text now came back to him eighteen years later and took hold of his heart. This time he surrendered. He made his vow in writing, "I offer myself up, soul and body, unto God. . . . I flee for shelter to the blood of Jesus. I will live to Him, I will die to Him . . . all I am and all I have are His."

That was on August 26, 1708. He liked to tell people, "That night I got my head out of time and into eternity."

From this crisis and conversion, God gave great power to his preaching, and thousands came weekly to hear him lift up Christ as Savior and Lord. Few men of that time enjoyed greater popularity.

Epilogue

Ten years after his conversion, Erskine preached a sermon on this passage. It was said that no sermon he ever preached made a greater impression on his congregation. It was printed and widely circulated and continued to be effective and fruitful.

After ministering in Portmoak for twenty-eight years, he moved to Stirling and served the Church of the Holy Rood where Mary, Queen of Scots, had been crowned when nine months old. It was also the church where King James VI was crowned.

While in Stirling he became the founder of the Scottish Secession Church, which objected to ministers being appointed by wealthy patrons.

When Erskine was seventy-three years old, an elder visited him in his final illness. The elder read scripture and prayed with him. He then asked Erskine what he was now doing with his soul.

Erskine replied, "I am doing with it what I did forty years ago; I am resting it on that word, 'I am the Lord thy God.' "

While his daughter was reading his printed sermon on this passage, he said, "That is the best sermon ever I preached!" A short time later he breathed his last.

Exodus 20:3-5

Thou shalt have no other gods before me. Thou shalt not make unto thee any graven image, or any likeness of anything that is in heaven above, or that is in the earth beneath, or that is in the water under the earth: Thou shalt not bow down thyself to them, nor serve them.

Conflict in Korea

"The students and faculty of every school in Korea must attend ceremonies at the State Shinto shrine nearest them," stated the order of the Japanese government. The year was 1936, and difficult times were ahead for the Christians in Korea.

"It is our civic duty as patriotic Korean citizens to attend the ceremonies," some church officials argued.

"Impossible!" declared others. "It is not simply a matter of being present and accounted for: Obeisance is to be done to the sun goddess, Amaretasu-Omi-Kami, patron saint of the Japanese army and mythical ancestress of the imperial household."

"The bow is compulsory and simply a patriotic gesture," some felt. "After all, if we don't do it, we face persecution and imprisonment."

"There can be absolutely no compromise!" declared T. Stanley Soltau, chairman of the executive committee of his mission. "The Word of God is clear: 'Thou shalt have no other gods. . . . Thou shalt not bow down to them.'

"We may lose our mission schools. Surely it is better to hold on to our property and keep our schools open," the opposition countered.

"We will close our schools rather than compromise!" Soltau insisted. He visited high government officials trying to get leniency for Christians but failed in his attempt.

The majority of the missionaries stood with Soltau, but as one by one the schools did close, the mission board back in the United States became concerned. They sided with those favoring compromise, fearing the loss of mission property.

This stirred up the opposition who again approached Soltau with their arguments, "God knows our circumstances. He knows the hearts of the students and faculty, that they are doing this from a good motive. Surely a token bow to an idol in a small shrine will not offend the true and reasonable God. The bending will be physical but not spiritual."

"Not so much as a nod of the head should be offered," Soltau insisted. "We can no more associate the worship of the sun goddess with the worship of Jesus Christ than it was possible in the days of Elijah to associate the worship of Baal with the worship of Jehovah. No true Christian will attend the Shinto ceremonies, regardless of the cost to property or life!"

In the middle of this controversy, Soltaus's furlough came due, and they headed for the United States. They traveled north to Vladivostok, where they would board the Trans-Siberian Express to go home by way of England. On the way, they passed through Syenchun, the Soltaus' first mission post. There they met several of the Korean Christians, among them Chinsoo Kim, one of his first converts who was now a pastor. He had lived for some years with the Soltaus, and he considered Stanley as his father.

"Father, I fear that we will experience hard times in our country," he said. "I don't know what will happen, nor what we may have to face. I will miss your leadership, but I will remember all the counsel you have given me."

"The Lord will sustain you," Soltau said. "I'll be praying for you that you will be strong to obey God's Word when you are faced with difficult decisions."

"Do you still believe we have taken the correct stand against shrine worship?" Chinsoo asked. "If we maintain our position, then some of us may suffer greatly. It must not be for less than the honor of Christ. I must know for sure that this is the issue."

"There is no question about it," Soltau affirmed. "God's Word is plain. We must have no other gods before Him. We must not bow down to them."

"Thank you," Chinsoo said with great emotion and pressed a letter into Soltau's hand.

Later in the train, Soltau opened the letter and read: "Of one thing I am certain, you will never feel ashamed of your son. Whatever comes, I am looking to the Lord for His enabling power, so that in all things I shall be faithful to Him and shall never deny Him or bring disgrace to His name."

Epilogue

An operation for a kidney stone kept Stanley Soltau and his family from returning to Korea as scheduled. By the time he was well enough to travel, World War II had started and they had to cancel plans to return. He pastored a church in Memphis, Tennessee, for a number of years and wrote a book about the establishment of national churches entitled *Missions at the Crossroads*.

In the next few years following Soltau's departure from Korea, at least sixty thousand Korean Christians were arrested and thrown into jail for their refusal to do obeisance to the sun goddess. Among them was Chinsoo.

Pastor Chinsoo was imprisoned at Pyongyang with many other Christians. When his wife was permitted to visit him after two years, he had been tortured so much that he didn't recognize her. She never saw him again. However, a friend of the family passed the jail one winter day, and seeing a pile of frozen corpses stacked like cordwood, went over to have a look. There he saw the icy face of Pastor Chinsoo, one of thousands who, strengthened by the Word of God, found power to refuse obeisance to a false god.

Esther 4:16

I will go in unto the king . . .
and if I perish, I perish.

Sawdust Surrender

Ellen Harmon was twelve years old when William Miller visited Portland, Maine, and presented a series of lectures on the second coming of Jesus. A spiritual awakening occurred among the people of various denominational backgrounds. Miller spoke with great power on the prophecies of Scripture and held the crowds spellbound.

Sinners were invited to come forward to the altar to experience the joy of forgiveness of sin. Ellen came with others, but she did not find the peace for which she was searching. She felt that she was not good enough to enter heaven and that such a benefit was too much for her to expect. For many months she wandered in darkness and unbelief.

Then when she was fourteen years old in the summer of 1842, Ellen went with her parents to a Methodist camp meeting in Buxton, Maine. She determined to earnestly seek the Lord there to see if she could find forgiveness of sin.

She was greatly encouraged to believe when she heard a minister speak on Esther 4:16: "I will go in unto the king . . . and if I perish, I perish."

The minister spoke to those wavering between hope and fear. He told them, "You are longing to be saved from your sins and receive the pardoning love of Jesus. Yet you are held captive by timidity and fear of failure. I urge you to surrender to God and trust His mercy without delay. As Ahasuerus extended to Esther the signal of his favor, so you will find a gracious Saviour ready to give to you the scepter of His mercy. You need only put forward the hand of faith and touch the scepter of His grace."

Through this Bible analogy, Ellen saw very clearly that there was hope for her. She saw what she must do to be saved. Ellen went forward to the altar earnestly seeking the forgiveness of her sins. She bowed with the others and cried out in her heart, *Help, Jesus, save me, or I perish.*

Suddenly her burden left her and her heart felt light. Jesus seemed very near to her. There was assurance in her heart.

One of the respected women came to her and said, "Dear child, have you found Jesus?"

Ellen was about to answer Yes when the sister said, "Indeed you have; I can see it in your face."

Ellen felt so happy that Jesus had blessed her and forgiven all her sins. Soon the camp meeting ended and they headed home. Ellen's mind was full of joyful thoughts. To her everything in nature seemed changed. The sun now shone bright and clear. The trees and grass were a fresher green, the sky a deeper blue. The birds sang more sweetly than ever before.

Epilogue

With her husband, James White, Ellen later became one of the pioneer leaders of the newly formed Seventh-day Adventist movement. In 1855 she and James moved to Battle Creek, Michigan, which became the headquarters of that denomination for the next fifty years.

Ellen became a prolific writer of periodical articles and books on health, education, and biblical lore. Her writings had a special inspiration to those who were encouraged by them. She seemed to have a particular power to draw her readers close to Jesus, no doubt drawn from her own conversion experience.

As a church leader she traveled both to Europe and Australia encouraging the development of the church in those lands. She lived until 1915, her eighty-eighth year.

Psalm 11:1, 3

In the Lord put I my trust . . .
If the foundations be destroyed,
what can the righteous do?

Singing on the Scaffold

Few lives have been more tragic than that of Mary Stuart, known in history as Mary Queen of Scots. Her father died when she was only six days old. Because her father was King James V of Scotland, on his death she became Queen of that highland realm. Five and a half years later, her mother sent her to France to be educated to rule Scotland as a good Catholic queen.

For the next ten years, Mary enjoyed the pleasures of the elegant French court. There she was said to be intelligent, charming, and graceful. She was engaged to be married to the heir to the throne, and many looked forward to a union of the Catholic kingdoms of France and Scotland. Indeed, loyal Catholics felt she had a stronger claim to England than did her cousin Elizabeth I, who had ascended to that throne.

Eight months after Elizabeth's accession, the English ambassador to France reported that he heard the heralds cry at Mary Stuart's approach, "Make way for the Queen of England."

Then after eighteen months of marriage, her husband died.

Realizing there was no future for her in France, she returned to Scotland. Her goal was to rule Scotland as a good Catholic queen should.

However, during her absence from Scotland the nobles there had declared for the Protestant faith. Led by John Knox, they no longer desired a Catholic queen to rule over them. Mary felt she could win them over with her grace and charm. Unfortunately, she lost the support of her cousin Elizabeth I of England by maintaining her claim to be the rightful queen of that land as well. Soon she lost the remaining support of her nobles in Scotland by unwise marriages and was forced to flee to England and Elizabeth's protection.

The Catholic powers of Europe had many plots with their English allies to remove Protestant Elizabeth from the throne. Several of those plots included killing Elizabeth. Mary Stuart was accused of taking part in these conspiracies, and the British parliament demanded that Elizabeth should sign her death warrant.

Elizabeth delayed her decision by three months. She knew her own life was endangered by these plots, but she was not sure Mary was involved in them. Besides, she had given her personal promise to protect her royal cousin. Finally, after three months of hesitation, Elizabeth signed the decree.

On the morning of February 8, 1587, three hundred English gentlemen gathered at Fotheringay Castle to witness the execution of a queen. Maintaining her innocence to the last, Mary, face covered with a white veil and holding an ivory crucifix in her hand, kneeled and repeated the eleventh Psalm.

"In the Lord put I my trust. . . . For, lo, the wicked bend their bow . . . that they may . . . shoot at the upright in heart. If the foundations be destroyed, what can the righteous do? . . . For the righteous Lord loveth righteousness; his countenance doth behold the upright."

She prayed then laid her head upon the block. Her severed head revealed that her hair had turned white. She was forty-four years old, having been captive in England for nineteen years.

Epilogue

Mary's son, James VI, who was a Protestant in faith, ruled Scotland at her death. Sixteen years later at the death of Elizabeth, he became James I of England. It was under his authority that the King James Version of the Bible was translated and published in England.

The body of Mary Queen of Scots is entombed in Westminster Abbey, not far from that of her cousin Queen Elizabeth I.

Psalm 23:1

The Lord is my shepherd;
I shall not want.

Island Hiding Place

It was early September, 1870. All eyes in the lobby of the fashionable hotel in Ryde, Isle of Wight, England, were on the newest arrival. It was evident she was one of the aristocracy. She held her auburn-crowned head high, and her blue eyes flashed authority as she walked in. Bellhops hurried to assist her and her fourteen-year-old son to their rooms.

"It's the Empress Eugénie of France!" someone explained. "She has fled here after the defeat of the French forces at the Battle of Sedan. There is talk of a revolution in France, and she's come here to protect the imperial prince."

The wealthy vacationers at the resort in Ryde had heard of the unexpected marriage of Napoleon III to the younger daughter of the Spanish grandee Don Cipriano Gusmán y Porto Carrero conde de Montijo and his American wife, Maria Manuela Kirkpatrick, a daughter of the U.S. consul at Malaga. Their marriage, celebrated with great pomp at Notre Dame in 1853, had been the talk of Europe.

Her beauty, elegance, and charm had contributed to the brilliance of the second French Empire that was now coming to an end. She had three times acted as regent during the absence of her husband and was often consulted on important questions. It had been she who had urged her husband to make demands of Prussia that resulted in the Franco-German War and the collapse of the empire that had caused her to flee to England with her son.

Eugénie could have come to no more peaceful place than the Isle of Wight. Its climate was pleasant and the countryside beautiful. From Ryde she could see miles of golden beaches, the sailing ships arriving from Portsmouth, and acres of woodland and green fields where sheep grazed peacefully.

However, Eugénie's heart was not at peace as she thought of the turmoil in France. She wondered what would become of her husband, who had been captured by the Germans. She worried much about him, for he had gone to battle ill from a bladder disease that made it difficult for him to move.

Alone in her room with her troubled thoughts, she picked up a Bible that she found there and opened it to Psalm 23 and read, "The Lord is my Shepherd, I shall not want. He maketh me to lie down in green pastures: he leadeth me beside the still waters."

Yes, she thought, *He has led me here to this peaceful island where we are safe. He is taking care of us as the shepherds care for the sheep I see on the distant hillsides.*

She continued to read, "Yea, though I walk through the valley of the shadow of death, I will fear no evil: for thou art with me; thy rod and thy staff they comfort me. Thou preparest a table before me in the presence of mine enemies."

She thought then of her husband, Napoleon III, ill, defeated, and in the hands of his enemies. She had a sudden assurance that all would be well with him and she would see him again.

Eugénie felt calmness flood her troubled heart, and for the first time in many days she was at peace. The words of Psalm 23 became her strength, her hope, and her anchor in her exile.

Epilogue

Napoleon III was released by the Germans and settled with Eugénie and their son at Camden Place, Chislehurst. There he underwent surgery for his bladder condition but did not recover. He died in 1873. Eugénie found a friend in Queen Victoria, whose own bereavements made her sympathetic with the exiled empress.

Six years later her twenty-three-year-old son was killed in the Zulu War. In 1890 she made a pilgrimage to the spot where he had fallen in battle. At Farnborough she built a church as a memorial to her husband and son.

Psalm 32:1

***Blessed is he whose transgression is forgiven,
whose sin is covered.***

A Poet Finds the Secret

Colonel James Oglethorpe heaved a sigh of satisfaction. At long last he had secured his charter from the king. His long-held dream of establishing a new colony on the south Atlantic coast of America was now practically a reality. He smiled to himself as he thought of the hundreds of poor Englishmen in jail for small debts and petty crimes for whom he had secured a new home and a fresh start in life. He thought, too, of the persecuted Protestants, like the Moravians in Germany and the Huguenots in France, for whom he could now provide a refuge.

Then suddenly an exciting idea entered his mind. He smiled again to himself. *I'll call the new colony Georgia in honor of King George II who has granted me the charter.*

Thus philanthropist James Oglethorpe was delighted when two brothers, John and Charles Wesley, agreed to go to Georgia as volunteer missionaries in 1735.

Charles Wesley, the youngest son of pious Suzanna Wesley, was her eighteenth child. At Oxford University he was one of the organizers of the "holy club" who were given the epithet "Methodists" because they disciplined themselves to regular prayer, Bible reading, and works of charity.

But Charles became ill in Georgia and had to return to England, his Christian mission a failure. Soon his brother John had to flee the colony in the dead of night and return also to his homeland.

However, in their travels to Georgia, these two earnestly religious men came in contact with the Moravians and became dissatisfied with their own lack of personal assurance.

Once in England again, they sought out Moravian Peter Bohler and questioned him about his religious faith. For several days they traveled together and heatedly argued with him.

Bohler held that peace and personal forgiveness were gifts God graciously gave when you found true faith in Jesus. The Wesleys argued that forgiveness and peace came as a reward for unceasing effort in the life of holiness.

During those days of discussion, Charles was again stricken with pleurisy and was expected to die.

Then John suddenly saw that, scripturally, Bohler was right. Saving faith did come in a moment and with it peace and assurance. He started to talk about such an experience and his need for it.

Charles became very upset that John would talk such harmful mischief. He was deeply offended and became so angry at his brother's stubbornness that he stormed out of the room.

But John's arrows had struck home, and Charles began to sense his own need for such a personal faith experience. After ten years of struggling for holiness without achieving it, Charles began to long for such a faith.

Charles was convinced he was dying but earnestly desired that he would not die until he experienced saving faith. For a week he lay in this anxious state. On Saturday night, May 20, John and his friends spent the night in prayer for Charles.

The next morning, a friend read to him the thirty-second Psalm. "Blessed is he whose transgression is forgiven, whose sin is covered," it began. In those moments Charles Wesley experienced saving faith and finally found himself at peace with God.

Epilogue

Three days later his brother John had his heart strangely warmed at a chapel in Aldersgate, and with the conversion of these two brothers, the Methodist movement was truly born.

Charles became a powerful preacher, but he is best remembered for the 8,000 hymns that he wrote. Four thousand of them were published. Some of his greatest hymns are "Hark! the Herald Angels Sing," "Love Divine, All Loves Excelling," "O, for a Thousand Tongues to Sing," "Jesus, Lover of My Soul," and "Christ the Lord Is Risen Today."

He wrote an average of three hymns a week for fifty-seven years.

Psalm 37:3

Trust in the Lord, and do good;
so shalt thou dwell in the land,
and verily thou shalt be fed.

*C*areer Crisis

At thirty-five, Frances Willard was at a turning point in her life. She had just resigned her position as dean of Northwestern Women's College, in Evanston, Illinois, over a governance issue. Suddenly free of responsibilities, she decided to travel east to study the temperance movement that was sweeping the country.

As if by magic, armies of women had filled the streets of towns in Ohio walking in procession, singing, praying, and speaking against the evils of alcohol. In fifty days, those women had closed down the liquor traffic and saloons in two hundred fifty towns and villages. Francis had longed to be with them but could not because of her duties at the university. Now she was free, and she decided to learn all she could about this grassroots movement of women that had now spread throughout eastern and midwestern United States.

In New York she visited the slums and saw the mission temperance work and was moved with compassion when she viewed the misery caused in families by alcohol. She attended the first gospel temperance camp meeting in Old Orchard, Maine, and listened to the stories of what women were doing for God.

While in a hotel in Portland, Maine, she came face to face with her financial situation. With no paycheck coming each month, her funds were running low. *If I continue my desire to help these women with the temperance cause, how will I meet the expenses for myself and my mother?* she wondered. *Do I dare continue with this crusade when I have no hope of income? Soon schools will reopen. Should I begin looking for another teaching job? Oh, God, what is it You want me to do?*

Her eyes fell upon a Bible lying on the table. A devoted Christian, she picked it up and leafed through it, looking for some word of direction for her life. She opened to Psalm 37 and began to read. When she reached verse 3 she knew she had the answer to her heart cry. She read it several times, "Trust in the Lord and do good; so shalt thou dwell in the land, and verily thou shalt be fed."

Later she said that it was this text that clinched her faith for this difficult emergency in her life. She knew that God wanted her to trust Him and to pursue a career with the temperance movement, but she had no idea how to get involved.

Going to Boston, she counseled with friends, pastors, and her own mother about her desires. They all tried to dissuade her. One pastor remarked, "If you were not dependent on your own exertions for the supply of current needs, I would say be a philanthropist, but of all work the temperance work pays least and you cannot afford to take it up. I therefore advise you to remain in your field of higher education."

Only one friend believed in her decision. Mary Livermore sent her a letter full of enthusiasm for her new line of work, predicting success if she would go as God was leading her.

While visiting in Cambridge, Massachusetts, Frances received two letters on the same day, both offering her a job. One was to be the principal of an elegant school for young ladies in New York City with a good salary. The other was from Louise Rounds of Chicago, begging her to take the presidency of the Chicago branch of the Women's

Christian Temperance Union. There was no mention of a salary. "The Lord has impressed me that you should do this work," Mrs. Rounds said.

Remembering the verse the Lord had given her in Psalm 37, Francis chose to "do good" and trust in the Lord "to be fed." Later when the women in Chicago offered her a small salary, she refused to accept it, so determined was she to allow God Himself to feed her.

When she refused the salary, the women assumed that she had some independent means that were being supplied to her. Francis did manage to eat, but there were many days when she had not even a nickel for car fare and walked many miles to reach her office. And there were times she went without a lunch because she had no money to buy bread.

Concerned about the health of her daughter, Madam Willard went to the women of the Chicago committee and told them her true state of affairs. It was then they insisted she accept the salary as a gift God had provided for her sustenance while she did His work. She accepted this time but felt ever after that she understood how many people in the slums felt when they were hungry and had no money. She was able to sympathize, as she might not have otherwise.

Epilogue

Frances Willard was present in Cleveland, Ohio, in November 1874 when women from all over the United States gathered to form a national organization of the Women's Christian Temperance Union.

She was elected at that meeting as national corresponding secretary. Although her name was considered as president, she refused to have her name on the ballot. Five years later, in 1879, she became the president of the national Women's Christian Temperance Union, an office she held until her death in 1898. She covered more than thirty thousand miles a year on her lecture tours crisscrossing the United States, averaging 400 lectures a year.

In 1883 she founded the World W.C.T.U. and was its president from 1891 to 1898. She was known not only as an advocate of temperance but of suffrage for women, the efforts of which eventually culminated in the Eighteenth and Nineteenth amendments to the U.S. Constitution. She wrote four books about the temperance cause and was the founder of *The Union Signal*, the national W.C.T.U. journal, and was its editor from 1892 to 1898.

For a few months Francis was associated with Dwight L. Moody in evangelistic meetings in Boston. She conducted daily Bible study classes for women. She was the first woman to be honored with a statue in Statuary Hall in Washington, D.C.

I am the Lord thy God, which brought thee out of the land of Egypt: open thy mouth wide, and I will fill it.

Faith to Feed Thousands

The life of George Müller has provided a fund of stories for generations of evangelical preachers that illustrate that God answers prayer.

The famed founder of homes for orphaned and destitute children in Britain's Bristol has inspired countless "faith missions" in a hundred countries by his experience of answered prayer.

As a lad growing up in Germany, he was tragically spoiled by his father's favoritism and lack of discipline. Before he was ten years old, he was a habitual thief who told elaborate lies to cover his stealing of his father's funds. Card playing, novel reading, and strong drink were his indulgences. The night his mother died, her fourteen-year-old son was reeling through the streets drunk. A year later he was arrested for debt and spent four weeks in prison.

When George was twenty, he attended a Moravian prayer meeting and was spiritually awakened. After this conversion, he gave himself enthusiastically to the service of his new Master as he had previously to his old.

Desiring now to study for the ministry under the evangelical professors at the University of Halle, his father refused to support him. He understood from this that he could be independent of man only by being more dependent upon God. He decided to accept no more money from his father. During the next two years of costly tuition at the university, he found that God supplied all he needed in answer to prayer.

He then traveled to London to receive training as a missionary to the Jews. Unable to continue due to sickness, he became the pastor of a small church in Devon, England. There he and his new bride found that the system of pastors receiving their salary through pew rents kept the poor from becoming church members. Together they decided to abolish pew rents, abandon his salary, and to trust in God through prayer for the supply of their financial needs.

Transferring to Bethel Chapel in Bristol, they continued to live by faith, receiving no set salary. There George Müller began to read the biography of the pietist professor at Halle University, August Francke. Francke had fed, clothed, and taught 2,000 orphans for 30 years in Germany 200 years before, depending on God alone to supply their needs.

Müller began to think that God might be calling him to do a similar work for Britain's orphans. At this time, Charles Dickens was writing novels about the plight of England's orphans.

Müller made this a subject of continued prayer. As he thought on this matter, he opened his Bible on December 5, 1835, to read from the psalms for his personal devotions.

He was forcefully arrested by these nine words of Psalm 81:10, "Open thy mouth wide, and I will fill it."

From that moment on, this text became one of his great life mottoes. He immediately began to pray that God would provide him a place to care for children, 1,000 pounds in money, and suitable helpers to take care of the children.

He soon discovered that he could rent the home he had been living in for the orphans. On December 10, a man and a woman offered their services to care for the children. One of the first gifts was 100 pounds from a poor, sickly seamstress. By April 21, the first orphans' house was opened.

During the next sixty-two years, Müller received one and a half million pounds through telling his needs to God alone in prayer. His institution has cared for more than ten thousand children. Five enormous houses were built for that purpose on Ashley Down on the outskirts of Bristol. So solidly were they built that they are still being used by the local education authority 150 years later. However, the Müller Homes for Children now operate in small family group homes.

Epilogue

Müller and his wife, Mary, also supported numerous "faith missionaries" in several countries in addition to caring for the orphans in Bristol. They provided great encouragement to Hudson and Maria Taylor and the great China Inland Mission program.

Numerous people have had their confidence in prayer renewed by learning of the experiences of George Müller. One doctor wrote him that his great achievement was "the most wonderful and complete refutation of skepticism."

When Müller was seventy years old, he and his second wife started on a worldwide preaching and mission tour. It lasted for seventeen years and included forty-two countries. His witness to the prayer-hearing God of the Bible through sermons, tracts, and books gives him a continuing influence among believers. He died at age ninety-three in 1898.

In 1996 the authors of this book visited Ramabai Patel's orphanage at Kedgaon in western India. Pandita Ramabai was inspired to care for orphaned girls in India by depending on God alone through prayer following the example of George Müller. Her institution for girls has already outlived her by more than seventy-five years.

Psalm 91:11

He shall give his angels charge over thee,
to keep thee in all thy ways

Facing Death at Sea

On November 23, 1892, Dwight L. Moody and his son Will lay on their bunks in their cabin on the German liner *Spree* because of bad weather. Suddenly there was a terrible crashing sound as though the ship had hit a rock. Jumping down from his bunk, Will ran for the door to investigate. In moments he was back with an explanation, "The propeller shaft has broken and the ship is sinking!"

Moody dressed and followed his son onto the deck where hundreds of anxious passengers milled around.

"There's no danger," Captain Willigerod assured them. "Go back to your cabins." When the second-class passengers tried to go back to their cabins, they discovered water rushing in.

By noon the captain announced, "The water is under control and we won't have to abandon ship. I expect we will drift into the way of another vessel by three in the afternoon." But it got dark and they had sighted no sails.

"That was an awful night, the darkest in all our lives," Dwight later reported. "No one dared sleep. . . . The agony and suspense were too great for words."

As the tense passengers waited, they saw rockets flame into the sky, but no one answered their signal for help. Sunday morning they were still afloat but drifting further from possible help. As the second night approached, Dwight got permission from the captain to hold a religious service.

They all came—Jews, Protestants, Catholics, and skeptics—looking to Dwight L. Moody for some words of hope. He clasped a pillar with one arm to steady himself and began to read Psalm 91, "He that dwelleth in the secret place of the most High shall abide under the shadow of the Almighty. I will say of the Lord, He is my refuge . . . in him will I trust. Surely he shall deliver thee. . . . Thou shalt not be afraid for the terror by night. . . . There shall no evil befall thee."

The eleventh verse touched Dwight deeply. His voice was full of emotion as he read: "He shall give his angels charge over thee, to keep thee in all thy ways." He had a sense of the presence of the heavenly messengers, and his heart was calmed in the midst of the storm. He prayed then, "Lord, still the raging of the sea and bring us to our desired haven. We are trusting in You to deliver us in our time of trouble."

Encouraged, he turned then to Psalm 107 and read verses 21-31. All eyes were fixed on him as he read verses 23 and onward. "They that go down to the sea in ships . . . these see the works of the Lord. . . . They reel to and fro, and stagger like a drunken man, and are at their wit's end. Then they cry unto the Lord in their trouble, and he bringeth them out of their distresses."

"Show me that in the Bible," a woman asked him afterward. When she read it for herself, she confessed, "I thought those were words you had written especially for this occasion."

Moody went then to his cabin and thought of his wife, children, friends, and his ministry on both sides of the Atlantic. He realized that the next hour might be his last.

He thought of the words he had read in Psalm 91:15, 16: "He shall call upon me, and I will answer him: I will be with him in trouble;

I will deliver him, and honour him. With long life will I satisfy him, and shew him my salvation." He cried then unto the Lord from the depth of his soul, "Lord save us, but thy will be done!" Peace came into his heart, and he slept.

At three o'clock in the morning, he awoke suddenly. It was his son calling, "Come on deck, Father. Come quickly!"

Moody followed Will onto the deck where he saw a small light rising and falling on the sea. It was the light of *Lake Huron*, a Canadian freighter that had seen their distress signals. They were on their way to rescue the 700 desperate passengers and crew on the vessel *Spree*.

There were some anxious moments as they tried to connect the two boats with a cable. Some felt the cables would snap and they would all go down with the ship. However, with the words of Psalm 91 in mind, Moody had no fear. He believed God would do as He had promised and would see them to safety.

Moody wrote, "There were storms all about us, but they came not nigh our broken ship. Seven days after the accident, by the good hand of our God upon us, we were able to hold a joyous thanksgiving service in the harbor of Queenstown." They had been towed a thousand miles to safety.

"Psalm 91 was a new psalm to me after that experience," testified Moody.

Will told his father, "I always doubted if direct answers to prayer ever came, but I am no longer doubtful."

Epilogue

Although a shoe salesman with only a few years of education, Moody is remembered as an evangelist who won thousands to Christ, inspired missionaries, and started three Bible schools.

During the 1882–1884 evangelistic tour in England, Dwight Lyman Moody spoke at Cambridge University, overcoming the ridicule of the students to win an unprecedented response. Seven young men of wealth, social position, and athletic prowess, known as the

"Cambridge Seven," gave up their careers and sailed the next year as missionaries to China. This was the beginning of the Student Volunteer Movement that stirred young people in the universities of the western world for several decades. C. T. Studd, one of those seven, founded Worldwide Evangelization Crusade, that sent out thousands of missionaries.

In 1886, Moody founded a school in Chicago that later became known as Moody Bible Institute. He also founded Northfield Seminary for girls and Mount Hermon School for boys near his home in Northfield, Massachusetts. He died in Northfield in 1899.

Psalm 107:43

***Whoso is wise, and will observe these things,
even they shall understand the lovingkindness of the Lord.***

*F*loating Treasure

Filled with excitement, twenty-four-year-old Alexander Duff and his new bride, Ann, climbed aboard the sailing ship *Lady Holland* bound for Calcutta. It was 1830, and the Church of Scotland had selected Alexander and Ann as its first missionaries to India.

Their assignment was to establish a college for the education of the native youth. He was to teach western science and the Bible. For this purpose he had gathered a library, large for that day, of 800 volumes. All 800 were safely stowed in the hold of the ship, and all 800 were lost at sea. Their vessel struck a reef in a storm somewhere off the Cape of Good Hope, South Africa.

Duff was praying in his cabin in the storm when the alarm sounded and they were ordered to abandon ship. His Bible was left on his bed as he hurried Ann to the lifeboat.

In the darkness of the night, their small lifeboat tossed helplessly about in the stormy waters. In the morning, someone spotted an unknown island, and they waded ashore. Without food or fuel, they erected a crude shelter of driftwood.

Then a sailor, walking the beach in search of fuel, spotted a curious object in the surf. It was a Bible. It had the name Alexander Duff written inside its cover. The sailor hurried to the shelter where the passengers were drying out. Dr. Duff opened the Bible on the sand in front of them and read Psalm 107. They especially noted the description of God's deliverance of sailors at sea in verses 23 to 31. The missionary gave special stress to verse 43, how they should be wise and understand the lovingkindness of the Lord in their deliverance at sea. The passengers thanked God and took courage.

Within a few hours, two islanders discovered them and brought them penguin eggs to eat. These men then rowed forty miles to the mainland to get help.

Epilogue

Securing passage on another vessel, the Duffs continued on their eight-month voyage, only to be shipwrecked a second time in the estuary of the Hooghly River, off Calcutta.

With the help of Brahman reformer Ram Mohan Roy, Duff opened a college in Calcutta that was effective in bringing a number of upper caste Hindus to faith in Christ.

That college proved to be the beginning of the University of Calcutta, which continues to educate thousands of students today.

Psalm 118:17

***I shall not die, but live,
and declare the works of the Lord.***

The Battle for the Bible

Six hundred years ago the people of England did not have the Bible in the English tongue. The educated and clergy had the Scriptures available in Latin or Norman French if they took the effort to find them. But only fragments of the Bible could be found in English.

Then John Wycliffe, the Morning Star of the Reformation, came on the scene. In the 1370s, this Oxford University professor came into prominence as the foremost scholar in Europe.

In his teens, as a student in college, Wycliffe began a serious study of the Scriptures in Latin. At this time the Black Death, or bubonic plague, swept Europe, killing two-thirds of the population in some places.

Alarmed that he was not ready to die, Wycliffe spent hours night and day alone in his room calling on God with sighs and groans. He was impressed to open the Scriptures. There he discovered the great teaching of salvation through faith in Jesus. He believed and was blessed. He began to teach it in the university and in the church.

Wycliffe demanded that the authority of Scripture be reestablished in the Christian church. This brought him into conflict with the clergy, the friars, and the head of the state church of Europe. He defended the right of the English Crown to resist taxation by Rome. He contended that the church's teaching that the bread and wine of Communion became the actual body and blood of Christ was not scriptural. Gregory XI in Rome issued five scathing bulls against Wycliffe demanding his condemnation.

In the midst of this conflict, at the age of fifty, he became dangerously ill. It appeared that he would die. His enemies saw an opportunity to frighten him into recanting the harm he had done to their teachings and influence.

A delegation of religious leaders and eldermen visited his sick bed to warn him. "You have death on your lips," they said. "Be touched by your faults, and retract."

His silence encouraged them that he would agree. But as he thought of death, he realized anew the power of the gospel. After a thoughtful pause, he sat up on his couch and with a piercing look repeated the words of Psalm 118:17. "I shall not die, but live. . . ." Then he added, "and again declare the evil deeds of the friars."

Encouraged by this powerful scripture, Wycliffe did recover and spent his next few years concentrating on his greatest work—translating the Bible into English.

Epilogue

Wycliffe and his assistants completed the New Testament in English in 1380 and the Old Testament two years later. His translation is the first in that language.

He then organized a group of poor Christians, known as Lollards, to travel throughout England teaching and reading the Scriptures to the common folk in their own tongue.

Wycliffe was condemned for heresy by the state church. Forty-four years after his death, his body was dug up and burned, and the ashes were thrown into the river.

But he is known today as the Morning Star of the Reformation. A few years after his death, John Huss of Prague republished Wycliffe's writings and began the Reformation there. One hundred fifty years later, Martin Luther was influenced by those writings in Germany. English scholars who fled their homeland in the persecutions of "Bloody Mary" Tudor studied Lutheran teachings and returned to England on the accession of Queen Elizabeth I to establish the Reformation there.

Wycliffe is also called "the father of English prose." This is due to the popularity and clarity of his writings and sermons in "middle English" from which the modern language was formed.

Psalm 121:1, 2

I will lift up mine eyes unto the hills,
from whence cometh my help.
My help cometh from the Lord,
which made heaven and earth.

Hiking at Gunpoint

"Keedee! Keedee!" The harsh words of her captors and the sting of their sticks on her back kept Debbie moving along the rocky stream bed.

Moments before, while on rounds at Ghindi Mission Hospital in Ethiopia, Debbie Dortzbach had been taken at gunpoint by members of the Eritrean Liberation Front along with a Dutch nurse, Anna. A shot rang out. Debbie glanced over her shoulder and saw Anna fall. She wanted to go back, but her captors prodded her forward.

Expecting any moment to feel a bullet in her back, Debbie cried out, "How can I keep going, God? . . . I can't . . . I can't. . . ." Tears blinded her eyes as she stumbled ahead.

They left the stream bed and began climbing a steep cliff. Debbie looked up to the mountain range ahead. Suddenly, words she had memorized long ago came back to her: "I will lift up my eyes to the hills . . . where does my help come from? My help comes from the Lord, the maker of heaven and earth."

The words filled her mind with hope and courage. "My help comes from the Lord!" Debbie repeated over and over as she resolutely placed one foot in front of the other, making herself keep up with her captors.

Later, when they stopped to make camp, Debbie repeated Psalm 91: "He who dwells in the shelter of the Most High will rest in the shadow of the Almighty. . . . I will say of the Lord, He is my refuge and my fortress, my God, in whom I trust!"

This began a pattern of recalling Scripture that kept Debbie strong through twenty-six days of captivity while she was held for ransom by the terrorists.

Epilogue

As soon as Debbie's husband, Karl, learned of the kidnapping, he went to the American consulate for help. Thousands of people around the world joined him in praying for her release.

Debbie was freed on June 22, 1974, after twenty-six days of captivity. A week later they flew home, arriving at JFK International Airport on July 2. They were met by hundreds of friends and relatives singing, "Praise God From Whom All Blessings Flow."

The same week, the mission hospital reopened. Five others taken captive when Debbie was were also freed.

Debbie, who was five months pregnant when kidnapped, gave birth to an eight-pound-fourteen-ounce boy on October 16, showing no signs of the ordeal he had been through with his mother. They named him Joshua, which means "the Lord is salvation."

Psalm 133:1

**Behold, how good and how pleasant it is
for breathren to dwell together in unity!**

*S*even Survivors

A. W. Greely was an American army officer and Arctic explorer. On short notice, in 1881, he was chosen to lead an Arctic expedition organized in the United States to celebrate the first International Circumpolar Year (1882–1883).

He commanded Fort Conger on Ellesmere Island with a party of twenty-five. It was the most northerly station for meteorological and magnetic observations. They explored a large amount of new terrain on Ellesmere Island and crossed over to the shore of Greenland, a journey of more than a thousand miles.

But their relief ships failed to reach them with supplies in either 1882 or 1883. Fort Conger was abandoned in August, and they sailed south in a steam launch with forty days' supply of food. On October 15 they reached Cape Sabine, 250 miles to the south. They improvised shelters and prepared to face 250 days of winter without further supplies of food.

The men arranged their time so as to have a religious service each Sunday. During their first such service, Greely arranged for

Psalm 133 to be read. He then spoke to them about the importance of working together, being friends with each other, and working to bring into unity those who might drift into unpleasantness and confrontation. Otherwise they could all perish.

They listened to the counsel of this passage of Scripture and sought to put it into practice in their camp.

Greely was able to record later: "For months without drinking water, destitute of warmth, with sleeping bags frozen to the ground, with walls, roof, and floor covered with frost and ice, deprived of sufficient light, heat, or food, they were never without courage, faith, and hope."

It is not unexpected that nineteen of the men died that winter. The remarkable thing was that seven, including their commander, were still alive when the rescue expedition reached them in June of 1884. Without the effort for unity spoken of in this passage, none could have survived.

Epilogue

Commander Greely later became the chief signal officer of the United States Army. Then he headed the United States Weather Service until 1891. He wrote extensively on scientific subjects and died in his ninety-first year in 1935.

Psalm 139:9, 10

If I take wings of the morning, and dwell in the uttermost parts of the sea, even there shall Thy hand lead me and Thy right hand shall hold me.

Whaleboat Rescue

On the afternoon of November 21, 1915, Sir Earnest Shackleton looked across the endless expanse of ice to where the ship that had brought them from England to Antarctica was wedged between ice floes—its bow shoved far down into the ice, her mainmast broken, her stern a dark mass against the whiteness.

After nine months of being stuck in the ice, the *Endurance* had been crushed by the pressure, and they had abandoned ship. They had been camped for several days on an ice floe ten feet thick and about a third of a mile across. They had tents, the clothes on their backs, three lifeboats, and what provisions they had been able to salvage from the wrecked boat.

As Shackleton stared at the stern of the *Endurance*, there was a sudden movement. He shouted, "She's going!" The twenty-seven other members of his expedition scrambled out of their tents. They watched as the stern rose into the air then disappeared, ice closing in where it had been.

For five and a half months they drifted on the ice floe more than three hundred miles from land. Several times the floe split beneath their feet. Blizzards howled around them, and the winds drove them toward open ocean. Able at last to launch their boats, they landed on Elephant Island a few days later.

Shackleton set out with five of his men in one of the twenty-foot open boats. They headed for South Georgia eight hundred miles away, where there was a whaling station. It was a grueling journey, taxing all their powers of endurance against the South Atlantic storms with their gale force winds and ninety-foot waves. When Shackleton and his men finally arrived, it was on the wrong side of the island.

In telling of that frightful trip of sixteen days, Shackleton often repeated words from Psalm 139:9, 10: "If I take the wings of the morning, and dwell in the uttermost parts of the sea; even there shall thy hand lead me, and thy right hand shall hold me."

Then he would add: "That psalm exactly fitted our case. Those words were a continual source of strength to me. We knew that there was Someone above taking care of us."

"I'll take Wolsey and Crean with me," Shackleton decided after they had landed. "We'll hike the twenty-nine miles to the station and come back to get you. It's 150 miles by water and our boat wouldn't make it."

The three men set out over some of the most dangerous terrain on the planet. They crossed ranges of razorback peaks and treacherous glaciers. No man since has been able to do what they did. In writing about that experience, Shackleton said, "When I look back upon those days, with all their anxiety and peril, I cannot doubt that our party was divinely guided, both over the snowfields and across the storm-swept sea. I know that, during that long and racking march of thirty-six hours over the unnamed mountains and glaciers of South Georgia, it seemed to me, very often, that we were four, not three!"

Wolsey said to Shackleton at the end of the ordeal, "Boss, I had a curious feeling on that march that there was another Person with us." Crean nodded agreement.

After four attempts at rescuing the twenty-two men left on Elephant Island, Shackleton finally succeeded. The men had been stranded for four months and five days with nothing to eat but penguins.

Epilogue

Sir Ernest Shackleton wrote of his ordeal in the book *South.* He set out on his final expedition in 1921 in *The Quest,* but he died on board ship in early 1922. He was buried on South Georgia Island.

Historians agree that what the explorer set out to do—cross the Antarctic Continent on foot—was not nearly so spectacular as the extraordinary feat he did accomplish in saving every man in his expedition.

It was written about him, "He was ambitious both for himself and for the honor of his country, but his outstanding characteristic was leadership. Courage, optimism, and endurance, colored by a streak of romanticism, earned him the trust and devotion of all his men under the most difficult circumstances."

**Trust in the Lord with all thine heart;
and lean not unto thine own understanding.
In all thy ways acknowledge him,
and he shall direct thy paths.**

Facing Bankruptcy

It was after midnight at the Orlando home of Walt Meloon, president of Correct Craft. He lay awake, tossing and turning, wrestling with his problem with the U.S. government inspector. If he didn't give the man a payoff, the rejections of boats for minor flaws would continue, and it could spell the end of his company.

It had been his assault boats that were used by Dwight D. Eisenhower's troops to bring down Adolf Hitler's armies in the closing days of World War II. His waterskiing boats were world famous. He currently held a contract with the government for 3,000 boats worth almost $100,000 each.

The problem was that the government inspector wanted to be paid twice for his travel expenses, once by the government, as well as by Meloon. This money he would put in his own pocket, a payoff for passing all the boats on the assembly line. Walt Meloon had refused to do it, feeling it was dishonest. As a result, the inspector began rejecting a large number of boats for minor flaws. If this kept up, Meloon would not be able to pay his creditors, and bankruptcy seemed the only way out.

Walt slipped out of bed and went to the living room. Placing his open Bible on a stool before him, he knelt to talk it over with the Lord. *You know the problem I'm facing, Lord. What am I to do? Show me what I should do.*

He opened his eyes then and began to read from the pages before him. The light of the living-room lamp fell on Proverbs 3:5, 6 and it seemed to Walt that they glowed brighter than all the rest: "Trust in the Lord with all thine heart; and lean not unto thine own understanding. In all thy ways acknowledge him; and he shall direct thy paths."

That's my answer, Lord, Walt thought. *To pay off the man would not be trusting You but rather giving in to the ways of the world. I will not do it. I believe You will see me through.*

Not long after that prayer, the inspector arrived just as forty already approved boats were ready to leave on a flatcar. "I don't like their looks," he said. "They've got to be unloaded and refinished."

At that point, Meloon knew his company was finished. He already owed more than a million dollars to 228 creditors, and he had no way to meet those commitments. He called all his creditors together and told them the story. They suggested he seek protection under chapter 11 of the Bankruptcy Act.

Things got worse at the factory. They had to let all their employees go. They began the long legal proceedings of filing bankruptcy, and it was eventually granted them with the stipulation that they pay 10 percent of what was owed their creditors. The rest was written off by the other companies as bad debts.

This didn't satisfy Walt Meloon. He felt the honest thing, the Christian thing, was to pay back his debts 100 percent. It took him twenty years, but he did it, paying back every cent owed. In some cases, the original creditor had died and he had to seek out an heir to receive the check. People were amazed that he would do this.

"I was flabbergasted to learn that someone remembered an obligation that goes back twenty-five years," one man wrote to Meloon.

"Many of the people working here today were mere youngsters at that time, and some are so young as to have not even been born."

By May 1, 1985, he had whittled the balance owed down to $50,000. On July 1 the new boat models would be ready to run and he would need all of his capital for manufacturing. He asked the Lord to help him clear his debts in June, having no idea how he could get the money.

It so happened that it was that very month that the Correct Craft sponsored water-ski team participated in the Super Bass III tournament. They had never won any prizes but did it to advertise their boats. That week in this world tournament near Jacksonville, Florida, their team won, receiving the world prize of $100,000. Half went to the team and half to the sponsoring company. Walt had the $50,000 he had prayed for and paid off the last cent owed.

Looking back, Walt Meloon knew that God had indeed been directing his paths as He had promised that night in his living room. He wrote, "The story of Moses' forty years in the wilderness didn't mean a thing to me until we spent years wandering under the cloud of bankruptcy. It was not the shortest route, but God has His purposes."

Epilogue

Walt Meloon wrote a book about his experience, *Saved From Bankruptcy.* Every person who became an owner of one of his boats received a copy of that book with the warranty.

Meanwhile, he and his family traveled the world, giving their testimony of what God can do when we trust in Him. The first time he told his story publicly, it was to a group of missionaries in Indonesia who needed $50,000 for a mission hospital. He shared his experience and urged them to trust God for the money as He had done. They did, and during the next two years the Lord sent them $100,000.

The Meloons have sponsored a number of retreats for people facing financial disaster. The people share their stories, hear his testimony, and go away determined to trust God.

Isaiah 26:3

***Thou wilt keep him in perfect peace,
whose mind is stayed on thee:
because he trusteth in thee.***

Shalom! Shalom!

One Sunday morning in August 1875 in the resort town of Harrogate, England, Edward Bikersteth and his family joined scores of others crossing the common, known as The Stray. They were all headed for the village church. He greeted several he had met during his vacation at the famous spa town.

I'm glad I don't have to preach today, the fifty-year-old clergyman thought as he settled into an empty pew of the ancient church. He had spent the last few days roaming the moorlands and dales of Yorkshire and soaking in the 200-year-old mineral baths. Already he felt rejuvenated from his year of duties as vicar of Christ Church, Hampstead, England, where he had served for the past twenty years.

Edward leaned forward as his colleague Canon Gibbon spoke on the text Isaiah 26:3, explaining that the original Hebrew version of the text reads "Thou wilt keep him in *peace, peace* whose mind is stayed on Thee." He said that the repetition in Hebrew conveys the idea of absolute perfection, or perfect peace.

After lunch, Edward visited Archdeacon Hill, an aged, dying relative. The old man was depressed and disturbed, unable to find rest. While listening to his complaints, the words of the morning's text came to Edward's mind. Opening a Bible to Isaiah 26:3 he read the words, explaining how God was promising him, even now, peace, perfect peace.

The old gentleman quieted at the words, closed his eyes, and dozed. Edward went to a nearby table, picked up a piece of paper, and wrote the words of a poem. The first line of each verse asked a question about life's disturbing realities. The second line gave the answer.

When his relative stirred, Edward read him the poem that began, "Peace, perfect peace—in this dark world of sin? The blood of Jesus whispers peace within." The old man smiled and nodded as the poem concluded, "Peace, perfect peace—our future all unknown? Jesus we know, and He is on the throne."

That afternoon when his family gathered for tea, he told his experience, then he shared the poem with them, never suspecting that it would one day become a well-known hymn.

Epilogue

Edward Henry Bickersteth, D.D., the author of twelve books of sermons, poetry, and hymns, is best known for *The Hymnal Companion to the Book of Common Prayer,* published in 1877. It became the most popular evangelical hymnal of Great Britain. The hymn "Peace, Perfect Peace" was among the hymns included.

He continued as vicar of Christ Church, Hampstead, for ten years after writing the hymn. In 1885 he was made dean of Gloucester and soon after the bishop of Exeter. He wrote a commentary on the New Testament and died on May 16, 1906.

Isaiah 43:2

**When thou passest through the waters, I will be with
thee; and through the rivers, they shall not overflow
thee: when thou walkest through the fire, thou shalt not
be burned; neither shall the flame kindle upon thee.**

Out of the Ashes

Doug Garber woke from a few hours rest at the truck stop on the
interstate highway. It was early morning; not yet dawn. Around him
the truckers were stirring and starting their engines.

Better freshen up, thought Doug, *get some breakfast, and be on
my way. I've got a long way to go with this load before I turn around
and head for home.*

Doug bowed his head to renew his consecration to the Lord in
whom he trusted. He prayed for his wife, Marla, and their three boys
at home. *My, it's hard to be away from my family,* he mused, *but with
three growing boys to feed, clothe, and educate, a man has to earn
his bread doing what a man does best.* Guiding an eighteen-wheeler
over America's highways was what Doug Garber did best.

Doug reached into his shirt pocket and took out his little leather
pocket Bible. He always kept it with him in the rig. *I wonder what
promise and encouragement the Lord has for me this morning,* he
thought. *I think I'll read a psalm or two to keep my mind on the right
road today.* He chuckled to himself. *It's not enough to guide your rig.*

A man on the road has to guide his mind in the straight and narrow too.

As he replaced the handy leather-bound Scripture in his pocket, he thought of his larger Bible at home. In a little while, Marla and the boys would be reading from that precious volume in family worship before they began their day.

That Bible was his favorite treasure. His dad, Bob, had given that as a gift to his mom, Nellie. For years Doug and his mom had read that Bible together. They had shared it in Bible study groups. Together they had underlined God's promises. When Doug thought of home, he thought of that Bible. When his mother had gotten a new Bible, she gave this familiar one to her son. When Doug married, he took that Bible to his new home, just down the way from his parents.

Together he and Marla had read and treasured the promises of that book. *My,* he thought, *I sure hope my three boys grow up loving the Word of God as I do.*

But Doug had a major shock waiting for him when he called home that cold winter evening. His wife did not answer. What was wrong? A recorded answer said, "This number is no longer in service."

Did Marla forget to pay the phone bill? Doug wondered. Quickly he dialed his mother's number.

"I've bad news for you, son," she said. "Your house burned down this afternoon. You've lost everything. But Marla and the boys are safe."

"Thank God!" exclaimed Doug. "But what are we going to do? Our furniture, our clothes, everything gone?"

"Don't worry, Doug. Your family is here for you. Friends and neighbors are already coming over with food, furniture, money, clothes, and whatever you need. God's not going to forsake you now."

"I know that, Mom, but what about my Bible?"

"That's gone too. Everything went up in flames," she said.

Doug rushed home to his family. The next few weeks were difficult ones, but they managed. Then one day, Marla was picking through the ashes of their ruined home and found—Doug's Bible. She excitedly rushed over to her in-laws' home. "Look what I found in the rubble, Mom!"

The old Bible was wet. Its leather covers were shriveled and brittle, but all the pages were there.

Mrs. Garber took a towel and began to soak up the moisture. Then she dried it in the oven at 150 degrees. Slowly it dried so the pages could be turned. When Doug came home with his eighteen-wheeler, Mom said excitedly, "Open it up. Just let it fall open."

The book opened to the prophecies of Isaiah and right there was a passage they had underlined—Isaiah 43:2. "When thou passest through the waters, I will be with thee; and through the rivers, they shall not overflow thee: when thou walkest through the fire, they shall not be burned; neither shall the flames kindle upon thee."

Isaiah 61:1-3

He hath sent me to bind up the brokenhearted . . .
to comfort all that mourn . . .
to give unto them beauty for ashes,
the oil of joy for mourning, the garment of praise for
the spirit of heaviness.

Courage in a Prison Camp

Darlene and Russell Diebler were serving as missionaries in New Guinea when World War II broke out. They were captured by the Japanese and kept in separate prison camps.

One Monday morning in November 1943, after Darlene had been separated from Russell for eighteen months, a friend came to Darlene's barracks. "Come for a walk with me," Mrs. Joustra said.

Darlene followed her to a grassy plot away from the barracks where they could have privacy. After a few moments of small talk about work, Mrs. Joustra took a deep breath and began, "I didn't really come to talk to you about work. I came to tell you that Russell has been very ill in Pare Pare." Then unable to control her emotions any longer, Mrs. Joustra began to sob.

Darlene grabbed the woman's shoulders and cried, "You don't mean he's gone! He's dead?"

Mrs. Joustra nodded. "He died three months ago. Only yesterday the chaplain brought the message. He asked me to tell you."

Darlene felt numb with sudden pain. It was more than she could comprehend. Her husband of only six years was dead. She would never see him again. Suddenly she felt her whole world had fallen apart. How could she go on without him? Walking away from her friend, needing desperately to be alone with her grief, she looked up to the sky and cried, "God, why?"

Blinded by her tears, stunned by her grief, Darlene found her way back to her barracks. She grasped the rung of the ladder leading to her bunk and leaned her forehead against it. She closed her eyes and tried to come to terms with the cold hopelessness she felt, knowing he was gone. *Oh, God, please. I don't know how I can take this,* she silently pled.

Taking a deep breath, Darlene gritted her teeth, determined not to collapse just yet. She had work to do. People were depending on her. There would be time later to grieve. Heavily, woodenly, she went through the motions of living that day, thankful at last when night came and the lights went out and she could be alone with her thoughts.

She lay face down on her mat, longing for a soft shoulder to lay her aching head upon and someone to put a comforting arm around her. *Lord, are You there?* her breaking heart cried out in the silence of the tropical night. *Do You see my pain? Do You care?*

Just then the Lord spoke quietly to her heart the words of Isaiah 61:1-3, words she had memorized long ago: "He hath sent me to bind up the brokenhearted, . . . to comfort all that mourn, . . . to give unto them beauty for ashes, the oil of joy for mourning, the garment of praise for the spirit of heaviness."

So real did His presence seem that she quietly poured out her sorrows to His listening ear, sensing that He took note of every word that she whispered. She knew He understood her oppressive sense of aloneness, the grief too deep for words. She sensed that He wept with her; that He cared.

About that night she later wrote, "I was learning to understand the comfort of the Holy Spirit. Sometime during the dark hours I slept. The sword of sorrow had pierced deep within me, but He had bathed the sword in oil."

Epilogue

After the end of the war, Darlene returned to California and her family to recover. The twenty-three pounds she had lost in prison returned slowly. Wherever she was called to go, she gave her testimony of God's presence and power in the prison camp.

In 1948 she married Gerald W. Rose, who was under appointment to mission work in New Guinea. Together they returned to the Wissel Lakes area where she had served with Russell. Later they pioneered work among the Dani tribe in the Baliem Valley and the lower Wahgi Valley of Papua New Guinea.

In 1978 they left Papua New Guinea to work in the Australian outback on a mission station five hours south of Darwin, in the Northern Territory, near the village of Larrimah.

Habakkuk 3:2

O Lord, revive thy work in the midst of the years,
in the midst of the years make known;
in wrath remember mercy.

Through Plague and Fire

Three hundred fifty years ago, a wealthy merchant prince lived in the city of London. In his early life he had been a devout Christian, a man of prayer. He had prayed earnestly for his own success in life, in finding a wife, at fathering a family. He had prayed, too, for his spiritual prosperity, that he would be a fervent disciple of Jesus who would honor Him in all things and work for the enlargement of Christ's kingdom. He asked God to make him a success in business. He was ardent. He was sincere.

Then love came into his life. He met the girl of his dreams and married her. Together they brought into the world four wonderful children, two girls and two boys. During those years he prospered in business beyond his expectations.

But in the experience of having his prayers answered, he forgot the Giver of all these gifts. His love for God grew cold, his love for personal devotions slackened. He became too busy.

He was now forty-seven and a man of substance in London business circles. Then by an unexpected illness of his wife, he suddenly became a widower with four motherless children. And how he loved and cherished those two beautiful daughters and two handsome sons.

Then on June 7, 1665, the bubonic plague was reported in London. One hundred thousand people in a city of 460,000 would soon be dead. At its climax, 7,000 plague deaths were recorded in a week.

With thousands of others, Walter Petherick fled the city with his four children. On door after door they saw red crosses and underneath, the words "Lord have mercy on us" marking the homes stricken by plague.

That Sunday in Twickenham, in his home outside the city, he accompanied his four children to worship in the local church. During the previous week, a day of fasting and prayer had been called for, and that day all the churches had services of humiliation and intercession, pleading with heaven for the plague to be stayed.

The minister spoke on the third chapter of Habakkuk. The second verse caught the merchant's attention: "O Lord, revive thy work in the midst of the years, in the midst of the years make known; in wrath remember mercy."

That evening for worship, he read this verse again to his children. But before he went to bed, he threw himself to his knees and pleaded with God for the lives of his children. The thought of cross after red cross on the homes stricken with plague was clearly in his mind. With the name of each of his daughters and sons on his lips, he pleaded with God to spare that child. "Spare her, O Lord," he cried. "Have pity upon my eldest daughter. Spare my older son Henry, my younger daughter, my younger son." Oh, how he pleaded with God that night.

Then suddenly a strange memory flooded his mind. He remembered those days many years ago when he had prayed like that earnestly and fervently. What had happened? He had acquired wealth. He had acquired things. His riches had made him poor. He had lost his intimate walk with God. He had allowed good things to crowd out the best.

What was it the Scripture said again? He rose from his knees and took down his Bible. He opened it again: "O Lord, revive thy work in the midst of the years." He was now in midlife, in the midst of his years. There was still hope. "Lord revive me in mid-life," he prayed. Peace came to his soul, and he slept.

A year and more passed by. Again it was a Sunday at Twickenham, outside London. September 2, 1666. At breakfast his older son, Henry, rushed into the room shouting, "Father, the city is on fire."

It was the day of the Great Fire of London. In the next four days, four-fifths of the city would be destroyed, including 13,600 homes and 87 churches and nearly every civic building.

As Walter Petherick looked out over the ocean of red flames sweeping the city, he realized that practically all of his earthly possessions would perish in that conflagration. But he was at peace. God had spared the lives of his four children in the Great Plague. His spiritual life had been renewed. The flames could take only the gifts but could not rob him of the Giver. He quietly slept that night remembering "Revive the work in the midst of the years . . . in wrath remember mercy."

Epilogue

Unexpectedly the fire did not destroy Walter Petherick's warehouses. They were in the one-fifth of the city that did not burn. The pestilence did not destroy his children; the flames did not destroy his goods. And the records show that he enjoyed long life, abounding wealth, great honors, and lived to enjoy his children's children. And through it all he enjoyed the fellowship of God and works of generosity for Christ's kingdom.

Ezekiel 33:8

When I say unto the wicked, . . . thou shalt surely die;
if thou dost not speak to warn the wicked from
his way, . . . his blood will I require at thine hand.

Before the Thunderbolt

Mildred Cable was teaching at a mission girls' school in Hwochou, China, when she sensed God calling her to reach the unevangelized people of the Gobi Desert. She and her two single companions, Evangeline and Francesca French, left the school they had founded and headed to Mongolia.

They settled in Suchow, the last town before the Chinese border, a town they dubbed "City of the Prodigals," where they ministered to some of the worst elements of society. This city inside the Great Wall served as the headquarters for roaming bandits who preyed upon caravans of merchants.

At one point a young rebel, a man known as General Thunderbolt, and his 3,000 men terrorized the countryside. The outlaws rode through the villages plundering, raping, and killing. They captured Mildred Cable and took her to the hideout of their general to treat his wounds. After he was better, she asked permission to leave. They granted it.

As she prepared to leave she thought, *I wonder if this is the pur-*

pose for which God brought me here. Then the words of Ezekiel 33:8 came clearly to mind: "When I say unto the wicked, . . . thou shalt surely die; if thou dost not speak to warn the wicked from his way, . . . his blood will I require at thine hand."

There it was—a direct command from the Lord. It was a call to obedience from the authoritative Word of God. Mildred knew that she must act upon that word. Choosing her best Bible, one with gold lettering, she wrapped it in bright-red paper. Taking the present with her, she went to face the Thunderbolt, though she realized her action might cost her her life.

"Great Man, we have received your hospitality for many weeks," Mildred said diplomatically. "I'm glad I could help you recover. This gift is of great value. It is the Word of the Living God."

The general rose to his feet and stared at Mildred with a frown on his hardened face.

"This Book warns men to prepare to meet God," she continued. "I beg you to repent of your evil ways. Please accept this Book. Read it; obey it. Accept the salvation it offers through Jesus Christ." There— she had done it. She stood quietly awaiting the Thundrbolt's reaction. All was silent. Mildred could feel her heart beating rapidly. Would he accept?

The general saluted, took her gift, and bowed. Turning, she walked from the room, her mission accomplished.

Epilogue

Mildred and her two companions then set out on a missionary journey through the villages of Mongolia, returning to Suchow in the late fall. On the way they preached in twelve towns and many hamlets. In each place they pasted up Christian posters on homes and temples. They recorded that they visited 2,700 homes to tend the sick, held 656 meetings, and sold 40,000 portions of Scripture.

The women worked in Mongolia from 1923 until 1936, when they had to leave because of political conditions. They returned to

England, where Mildred Cable and her friends coauthored several books: *Through Jade Gate and Central Asia, The Gobi Desert, The Book that Demands a Verdict, The Story of Topsy, Something Happened, The Making of a Pioneer, Towards Spiritual Maturity,* and *Ambassadors for Christ.*

Mildred Cable worked several years for the British and Foreign Bible Society and wrote a book about its work that was published after her death in 1952, *Why Not for the World?*

Mildred went to the Orient for the China Inland Mission in 1900, arriving just after the missionary who had inspired her to mission service was murdered in the Boxer Rebellion. She spent twenty-one years in China founding a model girls' school in Hwochou that had classes from kindergarten to a teachers' training department. This was followed by another fifteen years in Mongolia. Together she and her companions crossed the Gobi Desert at least five times "gossiping the gospel" as she put it. After returning to her homeland, she spent another sixteen years writing and speaking about the unevangelized peoples of Asia.

Is not this a brand plucked out of the fire?

The Runaway Shoemaker

Welsh evangelist Thomas Oliver did not have a very good start in life. By the time he was five years old, both his father and mother were dead. Having an extra mouth to feed was not welcomed by his uncles and aunts, and he was passed from one relative to another for the next few years, unappreciated and unloved. Then an uncle secured him a position as a shoemaker's apprentice, and the family was freed from his care.

By the time Thomas was eighteen years old, he was vile, godless, poor, in debt, and miserable, with a filthy tongue and evil habits. The people of Tregynon, Wales, did not want him around, and he was forced to leave their village.

Poverty-stricken, he reached the city of Bristol, hoping to make a new life for himself in the city. George Whitefield, the great Methodist revival preacher, was at the peak of his influence in Britain and America. He made a short visit to Bristol, and Thomas Oliver was in the congregation to hear him that night.

Whitefield preached on Zechariah 3:2, "Is not this a brand plucked out of the fire?" Those words spoke powerfully to Thomas Oliver that night, and he surrendered his life to Christ.

Later he would recall "When the sermon began I was certainly a dreadful enemy to God and to all that is good, and one of the most profligate and abandoned young men living, but by the time it was ended, I was become a new creature. . . . I broke off all my evil practices and forsook all my wicked and foolish companions without delay. I gave myself up to God and His service with my whole heart. Oh, what reason have I to say, 'Is not this a brand plucked from the burning?' "

Epilogue

Thomas Oliver's life was transformed. He returned to Tregynbon, worked, and repaid all his debts. Later he met John Wesley and became one of his circuit-riding preachers.

Despite ill health and persecution in many towns, Oliver rode on a colt throughout Britain, covering 100,000 miles in the next 46 years. For a time he assisted Wesley in his publishing work. During this time he composed the well-known hymn, "The God of Abraham Praise" *(SDA Hymnal,* no. 11*).*

He died suddenly in London in 1794 at the age of 74.

Matthew 6:14, 15

For if ye forgive men their trespasses,
your heavenly Father will also forgive you:
but if ye forgive not men their threspasses,
neither will your Father forgive your trespasses.

The Guard's Impossible Request

I hate that man! Corrie ten Boom's face hardened as she watched the former guard at Ravensbruck walk toward her after a church service in Munich. *That's the one in the shower room. I'll never forget his face!*

Corrie's knees felt weak as the scene came back to her—the pile of clothes, shivering, naked women walking before the mocking guards, her shame as she brushed past this particular guard. She wanted to run, but there was no time. Already he was before her, stretching out his hand.

"A fine message, Fraulein! How good it is to know, as you say, that all our sins are at the bottom of the sea!"

She fumbled in her pocketbook rather than take the outstretched hand. She was face to face with one of her captors, and her blood ran cold.

"You . . . you were a guard at Ravensbruck, weren't you?" Corrie asked. "I am sure I remember you. Do you remember me?"

"I was a guard there," the man admitted. "However, I don't remember you. There were so many women. I have become a Christian. I know God has forgiven me for the cruel things I did there, but I'd like to hear it from your lips. Fraulein, will you forgive me?"

Suddenly Corrie realized she had no control of the hate, bitterness, and anger in her heart. She could not forgive that man. The horrid memories were too strong.

For what seemed forever, she wrestled with her feelings. The words of Matthew 6:14 and 15 came to her: "If ye forgive men their trespasses, your heavenly Father will also forgive you: but if ye forgive not men their trespasses, neither will your Father forgive your trespasses."

Love this man, her enemy? Forgive him? How could she do it after all the evil she had seen him do?

Jesus help me! Corrie prayed. *I can lift my hand. I can do that much. You'll have to supply the feeling.*

Woodenly, mechanically, she thrust her hand into the one stretched out to her. And as she did, something incredible happened. She said, "The current started in my shoulder, raced down my arm, sprang into our joined hands. And then this healing warmth seemed to flood my whole being, bringing tears to my eyes."

"I forgive you, brother!" she cried. "With all my heart I forgive you."

Epilogue

After her release from the prison camp at the close of World War II, Corrie rented an abandoned concentration camp and turned it into a refugee home. She tore down the barbed wire and planted flowers, transforming it into a place of refuge and hope.

She traveled extensively for three decades, speaking about God's love and power to bring forgiveness and reconciliation, even among former enemies. Eastern Europe, the Soviet Union, Africa, Latin America, North America, New Zealand, and Southeast Asia welcomed her. During a three-month itinerary in South Korea, she spoke more than two hundred fifty times. She traveled to sixty-four countries in the thirty-three years after her release from Ravensbruck.

In 1971 her book, *The Hiding Place,* was published. It is the story of her experiences working in the Dutch underground movement to help save the Jews and her sufferings in Ravensbruck.

In 1974 a book of her experiences of worldwide public ministry came out. It was called *Tramp for the Lord.*

In 1977 she retired in California to "Shalom House," where she died six years later.

Today visitors to Amsterdam may visit the ten Boom house and try to fit into the small hidden passage where many hid when soldiers raided the house looking for Jews.

Matthew 6:33

But seek ye first the kingdom of God,
and his righteousness; and all these things
shall be added unto you.

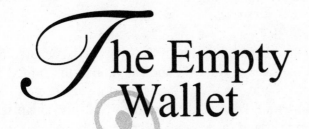

The Empty Wallet

Twenty-five-year-old Peter Marshall opened his worn brown leather billfold and studied the contents. There were three clippings of soccer games in which he had been the goalkeeper, a few business cards, two postcards of Scotland, various letters of recommendation, and enough money to buy his food for two weeks.

Peter had left his steady job at a machine shop in Scotland, had said Goodbye to family and friends, and had come to the United States because he believed this was what God wanted him to do.

When Peter stepped off the ship in New York on April 5, 1927, he didn't know how God would provide, but he was sure that God would. The young man couldn't foresee the wonderful way his heavenly Father would open doors of opportunity for him, but he did believe his mother's parting words. They came to him as he stood on the docks with his nearly empty wallet.

"Don't forget your verse, my laddie: 'Seek ye first the kingdom of God, and his righteousness; and all these things shall be added unto you.' Long ago I put you in the Lord's hands, and I won't be taking you away now. He will take care of you. Don't worry."

God did take care of Peter. He helped the young man to find suitable work. He impressed businessmen to back him for two years in the seminary. Once a department store called for Peter to come and pick out a suit that someone had paid for on his behalf. All through the depression years of the 1930s, there was money enough in his brown wallet to see him through.

Epilogue

Peter Marshall became pastor of the New York Avenue Presbyterian Church in Washington, D.C. and chaplain of the United States Senate.

Once in a sermon Peter said, "I can testify that through faith in God, through prayer and trust . . . my every need has been supplied."

He was a popular preacher, bringing crowds to hear his memorable sermons and prayers, some of which were published after his death under the title, *Mr. Jones, Meet the Master.* His widow, Catherine Marshall, wrote his biography, which was made into a widely circulated film, *A Man Called Peter.*

Senator Arthur H. Vandenberg paid tribute to him: "Dr. Marshall was a rugged Christian with dynamic faith . . . an eloquent and relentless crusader for righteousness in the lives of men and nations. He always spoke with courage, with deepest human understanding, and with stimulating hope. To know him was to love him."

Matthew 18:14

Even so it is not the will of your Father which is in heaven, that one of these little ones should perish.

Flames, Fear, and Faith

It was 3:00 a.m. on a January morning in 1974. The place was Oakland, California. Bob Searle, a rookie cop just out of police academy, was learning the ropes of police work from Frank, a seasoned officer.

They had just arrested a burglar and were writing out their report. Bob was pleased to be working under Frank. Frank seemed so self-assured and able to handle any situation. Bob was somewhat afraid at times, although excited by police work.

Frank kept drilling Bob on the importance of self-reliance. This confused Bob, because he was a new Christian believer and was learning to trust God. He wasn't sure how much he should depend on God and how much he should rely on his own resources.

As they shivered through their written report, they heard the screeching of tires and the crash of metal. A speeding truck had crashed into a car and knocked it through the side of an old wooden building.

The car started to burn. The flames reminded Bob of his fear of fire. Being trapped in flames was a recurring nightmare for him. But he ran toward the crash.

A man shouted at him, "Hurry, hurry, there's a woman pinned in the car."

Like a wave of sickness, panic passed through Bob. He soon reached the car, tried to open the passenger door, but found it jammed tight. He saw a woman trapped under the dashboard, unconscious. He was now sweating despite the cold of the early morning.

Bob and his partner tried every way they could to set her free. The fire was rapidly spreading. They could not get her out.

Frank backed out of the car shouting, "Get away from the car! Gas is spilling all over. Get out!"

Bob left the car for safety. His rescue attempt had failed. The car was filling with smoke. But Bob was horrified as he thought of the woman burning to death. His heart pounded wildly. "God, can't You save her? I can't do a thing!"

Just then a thought flashed into his mind, a quote from Matthew 18:14, "I wish that none perish."

God, he thought, *You aren't telling me to get back into that car are you?* He was terrified, but he knew he had to try one more time. He prayed, *Lord Jesus, you know I'm petrified of fire; You're going to have to be the One who does it.*

Taking a deep breath, he started for the burning car again. The fire stopped him from getting in on the driver's side. He ran around to the other side, praying. Somehow his fear was under control.

The door moved enough so he could get into the back seat. He knew he had to move fast before the gas tank exploded. Flames were burning the woman's hair. Large flames were on the dashboard. He bent over and lifted her up. He had her in his arms. He pushed her out the door. A passerby helped pull her. Twisting and pushing, he got himself out. Before they were twenty feet away, the car was engulfed in flames.

Publicly, he praised God to the people gathered around.

"There was no possible way humanly speaking we could get her out," Frank agreed.

Both knew that only God had enabled Bob to do it, and a powerful passage of Scripture had helped him overcome his fears.

Matthew 11:28

Come unto me all ye that labor and are heavy laden,
and I will give you rest.

A Veteran's Victory

Ben Harvey Carroll was a bitter and broken man. The American Civil War had just ended with Robert E. Lee's surrender at the courthouse in Appomattox, Virginia. It was 1865. Carroll was twenty-two years old, a wounded cripple on crutches. His heart was filled with disappointment, broken dreams, and doubts about God, the Bible, and the Christian religion.

Five years before, as a youth of seventeen, he had joined McCallough's Texas Rangers, then fought for the South in the war over slavery. The South had lost.

A child of Christian parents, Ben early began to doubt the inspiration of the Bible, the miracles of Jesus, and the truth of the Christian faith. In his early teens he read the Bible, marking what he saw were its contradictions and inconsistencies. He then began to read books by infidel authors such as Paine, Hume, and Voltaire. In college he studied Greek, Roman, and oriental philosophies.

When the war ended, Ben turned again to pagan philosophy to find some guidance for his future life. He found none. He suddenly realized that all the skeptics and anti-Christian philosophies had only negatives to offer. Nothing constructive or positive was there to give him hope, only darkness and despair. They left his heart cold. Death seemed to be the only prospect for a cessation of his suffering and pain.

He had sworn with an oath never to set foot inside a Christian church again. His father died believing his son to be lost. But his mother would not give up on Ben. One day she begged him for her sake to attend just one meeting. It was a Methodist camp meeting. He was not even slightly interested, but to please his mother he agreed to attend.

Ben did enjoy the music, but the preaching did not engage him at all. On Sunday morning at 11:00 a.m. the large wooden shed erected for the encampment was crowded. He stood on the outer edge of the crowd, leaning on his crutches, feeling tired and scornful. He found nothing in the sermon interesting to him.

Then the preacher startled Ben by asking a series of questions. They seemed to be directed to his state of mind. "You who stand aloof from Christianity and scorn us simple folks, what have you got? Answer honestly before God; have you found anything worth having where you are?"

Carroll's conscience responded without hesitation. *Nothing under the whole heaven—absolutely nothing.*

The preacher continued, "Is there anything else out there worth trying that has any promise in it?"

Carroll thought, *Nothing, absolutely nothing. All lead to a bottomless abyss.*

The preacher then spoke forth his challenge, "Well then, are you willing to test it? Have you the fairness and courage to try it? Put the Christian faith to a practical, experimental test. You, yourself, can evaluate the results. If you are willing to make such an experiment, and to begin it now, come forward."

Carroll was captivated by the idea. He immediately went forward with the others.

He was surprised by the response from the crowd. His hostility toward the Christian faith was known to many. His coming forward on such an appeal caused quite an excitement. Some shouted out, "Amen, praise the Lord, hallelujah!"

He decided to set the record straight. He stood up, and when he had their attention, he said, "I have not been converted. My heart is still as cold as ice. All I am saying is that I am willing to accept the preacher's challenge and make an experimental test of the truth and power of Christian faith."

The crowd became quiet.

The meeting closed, but Carroll felt he had not changed at all. He remained while some ladies sang their last selection. His heart was warmed by their music. Then suddenly, like a light from heaven, the words of Jesus' invitation in Matthew 11:28 flashed into his mind. "Come unto me, all ye that labor and are heavy laden, and I will give you rest."

In that moment he seemed to see Jesus standing before him. His face appeared to be reproaching and pleading tenderly at the same time. He seemed to be rebuking Carroll for going to all other sources for peace and rest but the right one. Included in that look was a gentle invitation to come even now to Him.

Carroll's response was immediate. In that moment he cast himself unreservedly at the feet of Jesus. In that moment the rest came—indescribable and unspeakable rest. During that night, the rest remained and brought him joy, brighter than the sunlight and sweeter than the song of birds.

Epilogue

Ordained to the ministry the year following his conversion in 1866, B. H. Carroll became a leading Southern Baptist preacher. Pastor of the Waco, Texas, Baptist Church for twenty-eight years from 1871–1899, he was known as a powerful preacher, keen debater, ready writer, and widely read historian.

He became founder and first president of the Southwestern Baptist Theological Seminary in Fort Worth, Texas, from 1910–1914. He was the author of forty books on religious topics.

Matthew 27:32

And as they came out, they found a man of Cyrene, Simon by name: him they compelled to bear his cross.

The Man They Didn't Want

Charles Simeon was only twenty-three years old when he was appointed chief pastor of Holy Trinity Church at Cambridge University. He served this influential Church of England parish for the next fifty-four years. From this pivotal pulpit, he influenced a whole generation of future pastors who served in the four corners of England and throughout the world.

In this period he helped firmly establish the evangelical party of ministers in the state-established Church of England. These became known as the "low church" party, who emphasized the preaching of the gospel, personal conversion to Christ, confidence in the inspiration of Scripture, personal prayer, and the devotional life.

Simeon himself had undergone conversion to Christ when he first entered the university as a student four years before. His main interest then had been horses, games, and dress. But by law he was required to take part in Holy Communion. He later said, "Satan himself was as fit to attend as I." In preparing himself for the service, he discovered Jesus as the substitutionary sacrifice for his sins and experienced a new birth.

But the university students and the townspeople of the congregation of Holy Trinity did not want Simeon to be their pastor. They wanted the assistant pastor instead. The students vigorously objected to his appointment and interrupted the services with noisy demonstrations.

They locked the doors to the pews so the worshipers had to stand in the aisles or sit on the free benches in the corners of the church. They insulted Simeon on the streets of Cambridge. This opposition occurred several times in the early years of his ministry.

What enabled this young pastor to endure these insults and continue as their pastor? One day, during this time of derision and contempt, he went out for a walk in a quiet place, carrying his New Testament with him. He prayed for some comforting word and opened his Bible. The first text to catch his eye was Matthew 27:32, "They found a man of Cyrene, Simon by name; him they compelled to bear his cross."

It struck him that Simon and Simeon are the same name. He felt like singing. He, Simeon, had been compelled to bear the cross through his present difficulties. What a privilege!

With this encouragement, he continued to provide loving care to the members, visiting the sick and ministering to the grieving. During a severe famine in 1788, he organized a bread-for-the-hungry campaign. Little by little he won their affection. Students were converted to Christ under his gospel preaching, and soon he had a large congregation of regular listeners.

Epilogue

Before Simeon's preaching and teaching ministry at Cambridge, graduates who became pastors had no specific training for ministry. He taught classes on the principles of preaching for forty-one years and published books on the subject.

At his urging, the Church Missionary Society was formed in 1799. Through this agency hundreds of missionaries were sent out by the

Church of England to India, Asia, and Africa.

He became a strong supporter of the British and Foreign Bible Society at its founding in 1804, at a time when many of the clergy looked upon it with suspicion.

He was influential in the establishing of the Religious Tract Society and the Church Mission to the Jews. He supported William Wilberforce in his campaign to abolish the slave trade.

In 1813, he began Friday evening conversation parties at his residence where students came for spiritual discussions. A vast number of his protegés later occupied pulpits throughout the British realm. These gatherings inspired many to become foreign missionaries.

He wrote and published twenty-one volumes of a series of suggested sermons on the whole of Scripture.

By the time he died in 1836 at the age of seventy-seven, he had become the most important figure in the evangelical party of the Anglican Church.

Matthew 28:20

And, lo, I am with you alway,
even unto the end of the world.

Facing Death in the South Seas

Thirty-eight-year-old John Gibson Paton followed Nowar into the darkness. The friendly chief on the island of Tanna, New Hebrides, led the pioneer missionary far into the bush to a large chestnut tree. "Climb up into it," Nowar said. "Remain there till the moon rises. You must not come down, because your enemies have threatened to kill you this night."

The year was 1862, and John Paton knew that they planned not only to kill him but to eat him according to their custom. He hastily climbed the tree and hid himself in the leafy branches.

He remained there for several hours listening to the frequent discharge of muskets and the hideous yells of the cannibals searching for him in the bushes nearby. Although his body ached, he knew he dare not move to betray his presence.

Writing of the experience afterward, he said, "Yet never, in all my sorrows, did my Lord draw nearer to me. I was alone, yet not alone. I would cheerfully spend many nights alone in such a tree to feel again my Saviour's spiritual presence as I felt it that night."

About midnight Paton heard the rustle of leaves and the soft tread of footsteps beneath him. "Come down now, Missi," whispered the messenger. Paton recognized Nowar's son. "It is safe now. Go to the beach."

Paton had no choice but to obey. About that perilous journey to the canoe that was waiting for him at the beach, John Paton wrote, "My life now hung by a very slender thread. But my comfort and joy sprang from the words *Lo, I am with you alway.* Pleading this promise, I followed my guide."

They reached the beach, just inside the harbor, at a beautiful white sandy bay. As they were ready to leave, the owner of the canoe tried to prevent their going. Finally, about daybreak the crisis passed, and they put out to sea, heading for another mission station on the other end of the island.

Part of their journey took them across country, and again they were surrounded by angry men intent on killing them. They encircled Paton and his company in a deadly ring, urging one another to strike the first blow or fire the first shot. Bravely, Paton broke through the circle and began walking down the path, the others following him.

The armed men ran alongside with their weapons ready, but none fired a shot. Afterward Paton declared, "I believe that the same Hand that restrained the lions from touching Daniel held back those men from hurting me."

They came to a stream, leapt across it, and disappeared into the bush. The armed men threw killing stones at them but did not pursue them. They arrived at the mission station.

Their pursuers then set fire to the church and the fence surrounding the mission station. There appeared to be no escape to the missionaries trapped inside. Then they heard a mighty roaring rushing sound, like the noise of a mighty engine. It was a fierce tornado bearing down upon the island. The wind took the flames away from the mission house. The black cloud opened, pouring torrents of rain on the mission station, extinguishing the flames. The warriors lowered their weapons. One of them exclaimed, "That is Jehovah's rain! Truly their God is fighting for them and helping them." They threw away their torches and disappeared into the bush. Soon afterward a rescue ship arrived, and the missionaries escaped to a safe island.

"I confess," wrote Paton, "that I often felt my brain reeling, my sight coming and going, and my knees smiting together when thus brought face to face with violent death. Still, I was never left without hearing that promise coming up through the darkness and the anguish in all its consoling and supporting power: *Lo, I am with you alway.*"

Epilogue

In fleeing Tanna, he had left behind all his possessions except his Bible and his translation of the New Testament into the language of the people of Tanna.

Paton went first to Australia and later to Scotland to make appeals for funds and missionaries for the South Seas. In 1864, he was made moderator of the General Synod of the Reformed Presbyterian Church.

Paton married a second time, his first wife, Mary, dying within a few weeks of their arrival on Tanna. In 1865 he married Margaret Robson, and they returned to New Hebrides, settling on Aniwa, an island near Tanna. He saw the whole island converted, and he gave them their first hymnal in their language. Later he gave them the New Testament he had translated into Aniwan. His son eventually resumed his father's work on Tanna, and the whole island was won for Christ.

John Gibson Paton's biography, edited by his brother James, came out in 1889, making him famous. Two years later he was awarded a doctorate of divinity by the University of Cambridge.

Paton spent his later years raising money for missions. It is reported that he raised more than $400,000 for South Pacific missions.

He died in 1907 and was buried in the Boroondara Cemetery in

Australia. On his tomb are inscribed the words of Matthew 28:20.

His son F. H. L. Paton wrote, "In his private conversation and in his public addresses, my father was constantly quoting the words, *Lo, I am with you alway,* as the inspiration of his quietness and confidence in time of danger, and of his hope in the face of human impossibilities. So much was this realized by his family that we decided to inscribe the text upon his tomb. . . . It seemed to all of us to sum up the essential element in his faith, and the supreme source of his courage and endurance."

John 6:37

***And him that cometh to me
I will in no wise cast out.***

A Book Born in Crisis

In a gloomy room of the Bedford County Jail, a man sat at a small table, his long red hair falling over bent shoulders. On the table in front of him stood an open book, a pen, and a flickering candle. Wearing the plain dark jacket and breeches of a Puritan, he seemed out of place among the ragged riffraff shouting and weeping around him in the crowded cell. No one seemed to pay any heed to him nor he to them.

John Bunyan, traveling tinker and itinerant preacher, had been an established fixture in the prison since his arrest in 1661 for preaching nonconformist doctrines.

He picked up his pen and wrote across the top of the notebook, "Grace Abounding to John Bunyan." He shook his head as he looked at it. With a quick stroke he crossed out his name and wrote "The Chief of Sinners." With a satisfied smile, he added a subtitle, "A Brief Relation of the Exceeding Mercy of God in Christ to His Poor Servant, John Bunyan."

Within the next few days, John Bunyan wrote of the struggle of nineteen years to find peace with God. Dr. J. W. Mackail, professor of poetry of Oxford University, called the result "the greatest of all spiritual biographies."

His struggles began at the age of nineteen when he married a wife who was a devoted Christian. She brought with her two books, which they read together in the evenings, *The Plain Man's Pathway to Heaven* and *The Practice of Piety,* which her godly father had left her when he died.

As a result of those books and his wife's encouragement, John began attending church, but it made little difference in his life, except to give him a sense of his great sinfulness and hopeless condition. After one particularly fiery sermon denouncing sports on Sundays, John reflected, *It is miserable to sin, and yet miserable not to sin!* To solve his dilemma, he decided to sin as much as possible and to enjoy it thoroughly. As he wrote in his autobiography, "I went on in sin with great greediness of mind."

This yielding to sin brought on a deep despair. He tried to pray and could not seem to penetrate the dark cloud of depression that hung over him.

"I fear I've committed the unpardonable sin," John told an elderly Christian friend. "I fear I have sinned against the Holy Spirit and there is now no hope for me."

The old man nodded sadly, "It appears to be so."

Greatly distressed, John turned to God, pleading for His mercy, but instead he heard Satan whisper to him, "Your sin is unpardonable. There is no use to pray."

"Still I will pray," John told the devil, and he continued for days agonizing before God. Writing about his spiritual battle, he said, "My soul was as a broken vessel, driven as with the winds. . . . I was as those that jostle against the rocks; more broken, scattered and rent."

One day as John was walking to a neighboring town, his anvil slung over his shoulder and a bag of tools in his hand, he contemplated his miserable condition. Passing toads on the dusty road, he thought, *I envy you little toads, for you can never know such misery as bows me down.*

Reaching the town, he sat down upon a wooden bench he found along the street. Laying his tools beside him, he placed his head in his hands and thought about his awful condition. The sun seemed suddenly shut from the heavens. He looked around him at the tiles on the houses and the stones on the street and felt that they were conspiring together to banish him out of the world.

I have sinned against my Saviour! he moaned. *I am finished! I am a lost man!*

Suddenly it seemed that the light spilled from the heavens and the words of John 6:37 burst upon his mind. "And Him that cometh to me, I will in no wise cast out." With a singing heart, John picked up his tools and went whistling on his way.

After that, whenever the clouds threatened to close around him, shutting out the light of God's presence, John remembered those words and was able to rise above his depression.

Once after his baptism, the cloud of darkness fell on him and made him miserable for three or four days. One evening as he was sitting by the fire staring at the flickering patterns it made on the walls, he thought he heard a voice within him saying, "I must go to Jesus."

"Wife, is there such a Bible verse that says, 'I must go to Jesus?' " he asked.

Bewildered, she shook her head, "I can't remember."

Thoughtfully John turned the pages of his well-worn Bible, seeing first one promise and then another. Then suddenly he cried out, "I know! I know!" The assurance of the afternoon on the wooden bench came back to him. The light once more broke through the clouds and John Bunyan knew that God accepted him.

Epilogue

Ten years later, while in prison for the third time, John must have had this experience in mind as he began to write *Pilgrim's Progress*. In the opening pages, he describes a man in rags, a heavy burden upon his back, greatly depressed, walking in the fields and crying, "What must I do to be saved?"

Evangelist points him to a shining light, urging him to go directly to it where he will find a gate. The miserable man approaches the gate and seeks entrance.

The gatekeeper replies, "We make no objections against any. Notwithstanding all that they have done before they come hither, they are in no wise cast out!"

Pilgrim's Progress, one of sixty books by Bunyan, was published in 1678 and became the most widely read book in the English language for the next two hundred years. It has been translated into hundreds of dialects and languages.

After John Bunyan was freed from prison in 1672, he pastored the Bedford Baptist Church until his death in 1688.

Romans 3:24, 25

Being justified freely by his grace through the redemption that is in Christ Jesus: whom God hath set forth to be a propitiation through faith in his blood, to declare his righteousness.

Coping With Mental Illness

As a small boy, Billie was guided through fears that darkened his nights by the care of an attentive mother. But she died when he was only six. This sensitive boy never fully recovered from the shock but was plagued by feelings of melancholy and loneliness until his own death sixty-two years later.

Several times in his later life he lapsed into mental illness, and several times he attempted suicide. But he also during these years left a major mark on the English literary scene, becoming one of the most widely read poets of England in the nineteenth century.

His religious hymns continue to be sung throughout the English-speaking world today. His name is William Cowper, pronounced "Kooper." Several of his hymns are considered classics of religious devotion. His most famous are "O, for a Closer Walk With God," "There Is a Fountain Filled With Blood," and "God Moves in a Mysterious Way."

A powerful passage of Scripture helped bring about Cowper's personal conversion to faith in Christ. It was this faith that helped him recover from periodic mental illness and to cope, though sometimes unsuccessfully, with his many disappointments in life.

A close relative arranged an appointment for him as a clerk or secretary in the British parliament. But Cowper, though educated as a lawyer, was unable to face the committee who was to do a perfunctory examination of him. He became so emotionally disturbed by the prospect that he became mentally ill and was taken to Dr. Cotton's private mental hospital at St. Alban's. Dr. Cotton was a kindly, cheerful believer, and under his sympathetic care Cowper began to feel better.

One morning, feeling somewhat cheerful, he enjoyed his breakfast, then sat in a chair, took his Bible, which he had refused to read earlier, and opened it to the book of Romans. There in the third chapter he read verses 24 and 25. "Being justified freely by His grace through the redemption that is in Christ Jesus: whom God hath set forth to be a propitiation through faith in His blood, to declare his righteousness."

Cowper says that on reading these verses, he immediately found strength to believe. He saw the sufficiency of the atonement Christ had made and believed he was pardoned through the blood.

In a moment he believed and received the gospel. He says he perceived the completeness of the justification Christ made for sinners on the cross.

Cowper recovered from his illness very quickly after this experience and was able to leave the hospital in June 1765 at the age of thirty-seven. Friends arranged for him to live in Huntingdon, near Cambridge, where his brother was a college don. To Cowper the village was like paradise, say his biographers, for his heart was full of unspeakable happiness of health after illness. At his first visit to the church for worship there, he was in such a spiritual ecstasy that he could hardly contain his joyful emotions.

Epilogue

Cowper's illness returned from time to time. But in his times of health, he wrote powerful poetry. He took up residence with a pastor's family named Unwin and lived with them for many years. They moved to Olney two years after he began to live with them. There he met John Newton, and they collaborated in producing and publishing the evangelical volume entitled *Olney Hymns*. Of the 348 in the collection, Cowper wrote 68.

He later wrote a ballad "The Diverting History of John Gilpin" that was soon a popular song in London. He gained acclaim for other poetry as well. His letters are considered some of the finest in English literature.

His faith in Christ and the Bible did not cure him from his mental illness but gave him the ability to cope with its periodic bouts.

His poem "The Castaway" is powerfully poignant and a classic of religious literature. He died in 1800.

Romans 6:23

*For the wages of sin is death:
but the gift of God is eternal
life through Jesus Christ our Lord.*

$\int$ alvation in One Minute

Ken Blanchard is the coauthor of the best-selling business book *The One-Minute Manager* and several other popular management volumes. *The One-Minute Manager* was on the *New York Times* bestseller list for three straight years in the early 1980s.

After graduating from college, Ken and his wife, Margie, became active in a local church in Athens, Ohio. Then the shooting of students at Kent State University demonstrating against the Vietnam War took place. Their pastor sympathized with the students and joined in the marches and demonstrations. His conservative congregation fired him. Ken and Margie felt it was done in a very un-Christianlike manner. They became disillusioned and angry and dropped out of regular participation in the church.

In 1979 they launched their own management consulting firm in California. A close friend started to urge Ken to renew his relationship with Christ. But Ken found the concept of original sin too negative for him.

At a Young Presidents' Organization convention he met Bill

Hybels, pastor of the Willow Creek Community Church, near Chicago. Bill told him, "I see a major difference between Christianity and religion. Religion is spelled 'do,' but Christianity is spelled 'done.' Religion is about the good things you do to deserve the favor of God. But Christianity is trusting in what Jesus has done for you."

Hybels urged Ken to find a personal relationship with Jesus. "Jesus will not only forgive you, but He will become your Guide and personal Friend," he promised.

Ken hesitated to make a commitment to Christ because he was afraid he'd fail, that he wouldn't be able to follow through.

Bill countered, "Receiving Christ is not about commitment and follow-through but about accepting salvation and forgiveness as a gift." He then quoted Romans 6:23, "The gift of God is eternal life in Jesus Christ our Lord."

Ken was not yet willing to trust Christ. But about a year later, he faced a major conflict in his business. He couldn't solve the problem, and he knew it; but he did not know what to do. He thought about what Hybels had told him. He realized he needed God's help, and all he could do was ask for it and accept the gift. Ken bowed his head and told God, "I can't save myself here. I can't solve problems like this without Your help. I accept Jesus as my Saviour."

When Ken said those words, a great peace came over him, and he knew he was a changed man. With the help of the Lord, he faced his big conflict and solved it. His wife and friends noticed the change in him immediately. He was a new man.

Epilogue

Blanchard Training and Development has become one of the world's leading business-consulting companies.

Ken has gone on to coauthor such books as *The One-Minute Manager, The Power of Ethical Management, Raving Fans, Empowerment Takes More Than a Minute, Mission Possible,* and *Managing by Values.*

*And we know that all things work together for good
to them that love God, to them who are
called according to his purpose.*

The Longest Weekend

It was Friday. Evelyn and Chris Christianson were driving from Minnesota to Illinois to speak at a prayer conference. Evelyn was driving while Chris dozed beside her. As the miles sped by, she thought over the events of the last couple of days.

During Chris's routine medical checkup, the doctor had discovered a little lump that looked suspicious. A biopsy proved that it was malignant.

Chris has cancer, Evelyn realized. Even the thought of it sent chills through her body. Visions of suffering, chemotherapy, radiation, and death clouded her mind. *No, God! Not my wonderful husband! How can this be?*

"Come back on Monday," the doctor said. "I'll schedule you for a CT scan, and we'll test your blood and bone marrow. Then we'll know if the cancer has spread to other parts of the body."

Monday seemed an eternity away. *What does our future hold?* Evelyn wondered. Then her thoughts naturally turned to God in prayer. *Lord, do You have some message for me to see me through this weekend? It seems so long to wait, and we don't know what the outcome will be.*

Romans 8:28 came immediately to mind. It had been her special text since she had miscarried during her first three pregnancies forty-two years earlier.

"No, Lord, not *that* old one again!" Evelyn cried out in disappointment and frustration. She longed for some new promise to give her hope, something grand and glorious to see her through.

Evelyn didn't hear an audible voice, but she did sense God speaking a message to her heart. He said, "Evelyn, I want to expand your understanding of this verse. You have thought that you will see Me working all things for your good when you get to heaven and view things from My perspective. But I'm telling you in advance, before Chris even takes the tests next Monday, that I am working for your good whatever the outcome is."

Tears coursed down her cheeks as she felt a wonderful peace and realized she could trust God even before they knew the outcome; that He would work through the circumstances for their good. The peace stayed with her through the long weekend as she ministered to others at the prayer conference.

On Monday, the tests revealed that the cancer had not spread. Chris had surgery, and his recovery was rapid and remarkable.

Three weeks later, Evelyn had to undergo a cancer test herself. While she was waiting for her mammogram, she focused again on God's promise in Romans 8:28. She felt a strong assurance that God was working out His purpose in her life, whatever the outcome would be.

Evelyn writes about that morning: "Immediately, all the tension drained from my body as His peace flooded me. I felt the incredible sense of being completely engulfed in a soft spherical capsule, in the rare atmosphere of God Himself." The mammogram showed no signs of cancer.

Epilogue

Evelyn Christianson is the founder of United Prayer Ministries, in St. Paul, Minnesota, and has been a speaker at prayer conferences and women's retreats in many countries. She has served as a board member on Chuck Colson's Prison Fellowship.

Her first two books *What Happens When Women Pray* and *Lord, Change Me!* sold over two million copies. She has also written the book *What Happens When God Answers* and *Gaining Through Losing.*

In 1980 the Religious Heritage Association of America named her Churchwoman of the Year.

Romans 8:31

If God be for us,
who can be against us?

Dearer to Her Than Life

Margaret lived in Scotland in the sixteenth century when Covenanters, followers of John Knox, were thrown into prison, and many were martyred for their faith. Margaret was a Covenanter who ended up in jail for nothing more than belief in the Scriptures.

There she became friends with Mrs. Lauchlison, a fellow Covenanter who insisted on obeying Scripture rather than the king's religion. The two encouraged one another in their cell, quoting Bible verses and praying for strength to endure to the end.

The day came when soldiers tied the hands of Mrs. Lauchlison and led her away to her execution. "Let me go too!" Margaret begged. Guarded by soldiers, she walked beside her friend to the beach where a wooden stake already stood at the water's edge. Margaret watched as they bound her friend to the wooden pole. She stared as the tide came in, slowly raising the water level about the woman tied to the stake. Each wave brought the water higher about her body.

"What has the old woman done?" someone cried out of the crowd.

"She was found on her knees in prayer," a guard answered.

As Margaret kept staring at her friend, the old woman's wrinkled face seemed aglow with heavenly light. Margaret strained to catch her words above the crash of the waves. "I have promised to obey Thee, heavenly Father. Help me now when I am tested."

The faint strains of a hymn sounded above the pounding waves. Margaret watched as they washed over the old woman's head. *Lord, help me to be as faithful to Your Word,* she breathed a silent prayer of commitment.

The next day Margaret was the one tied to the stake. As the tide came in, she recited Romans 8:31-39: "If God be for us, who can be against us? Who can divide us from the love of Christ?. . . For I am persuaded that neither death, nor life, nor angels, nor principalities, nor powers, nor things present, nor things to come, nor height, nor depth, nor any other creature, shall be able to separate us from the love of God, which is in Christ Jesus our Lord."

Epilogue

Covenanters were Scottish Presbyterians during the seventeenth century who pledged themselves to certain covenants to maintain their chosen forms of church government and worship. They were followers of reformer John Knox. A religious settlement forced upon Scotland in 1660 by Charles II did not satisfy the staunch Covenanters. For twenty-five years there was extreme persecution. Many suffered martyrdom, which ended when James VII issued the Proclamation of Indulgence in 1687.

1 Corinthians 10:13

There hath no temptation taken you but such is
common to man: but God is faithful,
who will not suffer you to be tempted above
that you ar able; but will with the temptation
also make a way to escape that ye may be able to bear it.

He Could Not Call God a Liar

Walking in his father's footsteps was the furthest thing from his mind. Franklin Graham was not at all comfortable being the eldest son of world-renowned evangelist Billy Graham. By the time he was in his twenties, he was smoking, drinking alcohol, and experiencing confrontations with the police. Finally at the age of twenty-two, in a Jerusalem hotel room, the prodigal son came home. He gave his heart to Christ and was born again.

The same night that he was converted, he came under conviction that God wanted him to give up smoking. He took his two packets of cigarettes and threw them in the trash.

He made it through the next two days without smoking, but on the third morning Franklin woke up with an overwhelming desire for a cigarette. The craving was so strong throughout that day that he thought about it whenever he was alone. He felt like tobacco had gripped him like the jaws of a junkyard watchdog. But he refused to give in. To distract himself from the temptation, he went to the Intercontinental Hotel to talk with Roy Gustafson, a family friend.

They sat together at the counter in the hotel coffee shop. Franklin told Roy that he was determined to stop smoking, that he had given all his life to Christ including this nasty habit. But he felt he could not hold out any longer. The temptation was too strong. He didn't have the power to withstand it.

Roy responded, "Oh, you don't, huh? Why don't you just get down on your knees and tell God He's a liar?"

"What? I can't do that!" Franklin said. He wondered what Roy had been smoking to say such a thing.

"Sure you can. Tell God He's a liar."

"What do you mean?"

Roy then repeated for him the powerful passage of 1 Corinthians 10:13: "There hath no temptation taken you but such is common to man: but God is faithful, who will not suffer you to be tempted above that ye are able; but will with the temptation also make a way to escape, that ye may be able to bear it."

Franklin responded, "That's great, Roy, but I want a cigarette so bad!"

"See, you prayed and committed yourself to God, but it didn't work," Roy said. He looked hard into Franklin's eyes, paused a moment, then leaned toward him and said, "So you need to tell God He's a liar. You've claimed that verse, and it didn't work."

"No, I'm not going to call God a liar! Besides, I haven't claimed that verse yet!"

Roy sounded surprised, "You haven't? Why don't you do it, then? Try and see if it works. What have you got to lose?"

Franklin knew that his friend Roy was speaking the truth. He had not really wanted an escape, just an excuse to take another cigarette. He rushed to his room and knelt by his bed and asked the Lord to strengthen him and remove the terrible desire to smoke. He made it through that day.

The next day, on a flight to Athens, the powerful yearning for a cigarette hit him again. He bought a packet of French cigarettes from a flight attendant and went to the smoking section of the plane. He lighted up and took a couple of puffs, but the tobacco tasted bad in his mouth. He threw the cigarettes away and was amazed that God had taken the taste of the habit from his mouth.

He quickly bowed his head and asked God's forgiveness for giving in to the temptation this once. From that day on, he never took tobacco into his mouth again.

Epilogue

Five years after this experience, Franklin Graham became the president of Samaritan's Purse, a Christian relief and evangelism organization. He also became president of World Medical Mission, which arranges for physicians to go on short-term medical missionary trips to needy areas of the world. A few years later, he was also elected to head the Billy Graham Evangelistic Association in succession to his father.

2 Corinthians 12:9

My grace is sufficient for thee:
for my strength is made perfect in weakness.

A Washerwoman's Faith

Amanda Smith was born a slave near the beginning of the nineteenth century, one of a family of thirteen. She lived through the deaths of several children, abandonment by her first husband, and the instability of her second husband. After his death, she heard God's call to preach.

Amanda Smith was an unusual sight in post-Civil War America. She was a black woman evangelist, traveling the country without salary or sponsorship, singing or preaching wherever she was called.

One well-known individual of that time said about Amanda Smith: "She is a Christian of the highest type, and as a simple confiding child of God has no superior among any women of our time." A minister who knew Amanda well referred to her as "God's image carved in ebony."

In 1870 she decided to attend the African Methodist Episcopal Church General Conference session, the first to be held south of the Mason-Dixon line, in Nashville, Tennessee. Women delegates were not permitted, but she felt God wanted her there, so she went. However, it was not without a certain amount of fear and trembling.

She feared that racial hostilities might break out and that she might be the cause for violence. She got on her knees to ask God what to do.

"You know Lord I'm willing to go wherever you want me to go," she prayed. "If you want me to die there for you, I am willing to do that. Lord, help me. Give me the grace and enable me to do it."

In the quietness of the moment, Amanda heard a voice speaking quietly to her heart, "My grace is sufficient for thee."

Amanda rose from her knees smiling. Her fear was gone. She knew the Lord would go with her to strengthen and protect her. However, once there, she faced not racial hostilities but hostilities of fellow church members.

Little groups gathered around the meeting place whispering about her, "Who is she? Why is she here?"

"She's a preacher woman," someone answered with disdain. "She's come to agitate the question of the ordination of women," several decided. But that was not true.

When Amanda heard their accusations, she replied, "The thought of ordination had never once entered my mind, for I had received my ordination from Him, Who said, 'Ye have not chosen Me, but I have chosen you, and ordained you, that you might go and bring forth fruit.'"

In 1876 Amanda was called to go to England, but she at first refused. *Who am I to go to England,* she thought. *It is OK for swell people to go, but not for me. I'm only a washerwoman. Surely God will not send me.*

However, it became clear to Amanda that God was calling her and that she must go. When God miraculously supplied the money for her trip, she knew she had to go even though she realized she was afraid of the long trip across the Atlantic. Once again God's Word gave her assurance, "My grace is sufficient for thee: for my strength is made perfect in weakness."

Amanda spoke at the annual evangelical convention in Keswick.

From there she traveled for almost two years, preaching throughout England and Scotland. Entertaining Amanda Smith became very fashionable, and crowds flocked to hear her sing and give her testimony.

Once when she stood to sing before an audience of women of rank and wealth, she suddenly realized that she was only a washerwoman with but two years of education, and she began to tremble. What was she doing here among people from the highest circles of British society?

As before, God gave her courage, promising her, "My grace is sufficient for thee: for my strength is made perfect in weakness."

Amanda told herself, *I belong to royalty and am well acquainted with the King of kings and am better known and better understood among the great family above than I am on earth. His grace is sufficient.*

She took a deep breath, walking out into the spotlight, confident that God's grace was enough to see her through.

Epilogue

In 1879 Amanda Smith went on a preaching mission to India. About his encounter with Amanda in India, Bishop James Thoburn wrote, "The penetrating power of discernment which she possessed in so large a degree impressed me more and more the longer I knew her, indeed, through my association with her I learned many valuable lessons, more that has been of actual value to me as a preacher of Christian truth, than from any other person I ever met."

She then spent eight years in Liberia, the African colony where many former American slaves had been relocated, where she helped to organize the Gospel Temperance Band. She also organized women's prayer groups and children's groups. While there she became ill with repeated episodes of fever and illness and was forced to retire from her missionary work.

In 1892 Amanda Smith retired near Chicago, where she wrote a book about the miracles God had worked in her life. She opened the Amanda Smith Children's Home in 1899 using royalties from her book. She died in 1915.

Philippians 4:4

Rejoice in the Lord alway:
and again I say, Rejoice.

Light in Her Darkest Night

Catherine Marshall LeSourd stood beside the heat table where her six-week-old granddaughter, Amy Catherine, struggled for life.

Her eyes traced the network of tubes attached to the baby's frail body. *Oh, God, heal her!* Catherine prayed silently. *You are our only hope!*

Catherine thought of the hundreds of friends who were praying for Amy Catherine. Surely God would answer such a multitude of prayers! She smiled with hope as the nurse placed the baby in her arms to hold for a few moments.

Suddenly the baby began to cry. The nurse looked at the heart monitor. "We have to put her back on the table now," she insisted and left the room in search of a doctor. In moments he was there bending over the baby. Then he shook his head.

"She's gone," he said softly. "I'm sorry."

No! It can't be! Catherine's heart refused to believe it. *God, please let it not be true. She can't be dead!*

But she was. Catherine had believed with great assurance that

God would heal Amy Catherine, and now the end had come. There would be no healing, no answered prayer, no rejoicing about the wonderful miracle God had performed. It was over.

The darkness closed around Catherine, and she could not pray. God seemed so far away. For weeks she struggled with grief, depression, anger, and sleeplessness. She agonized over the reason why God would allow such a thing after she had been so sure it was His will for Amy Catherine to live.

Is God punishing me for some sin? she wondered. *After all these years of thinking I was so close to God, why is He now so far away? What have I done? Why did God refuse our request for healing? How could He turn His back on me? I just don't understand.*

"Maybe that's your problem, Catherine," a friend suggested one evening. "Maybe it is your insistence that you must understand."

Catherine was startled, but the more she thought about it, the more she could see that might be her problem. The next morning when she awoke she had a desire to open her Bible for the first time in many weeks. She turned to Isaiah 53 and read of the sufferings of Jesus.

Jesus didn't understand either! she suddenly realized. *He felt completely forsaken in His time of pain. The disciples didn't understand. They, too, felt let down by God. This has been my mistake, thinking I could understand God, could know what He should do in the case of Amy Catherine.*

Catherine fell to her knees asking God to forgive her arrogance. "I need You, God!" she cried. "I don't need to understand; but I do need Your presence in my life."

Even after that experience, she still struggled with sleeplessness and emptiness of soul. She tried to reestablish her connection with God but often felt that He was still far from her.

Then one morning as dark thoughts filled her mind during her morning quiet time, the words of Philippians 4:4 came to her with the force of a command. "Rejoice in the Lord alway."

Catherine felt impressed that the Lord wanted her to get up an hour earlier each morning, at six instead of seven, to spend that time rejoicing in the Lord, praising Him with a grateful heart. She was to thank Him, even for all of the things that had gone wrong in her life.

This was not easy for Catherine to do. The next morning she felt as heavy-hearted as before. She still groped in the darkness of depression, but she was determined to rejoice as God had told her to do.

No praise came to her mind, so she opened her Bible to Psalm 66 and began to read, "Make a joyful noise unto God, all ye lands: Sing forth the honor of his name: make his praise glorious."

Catherine tried, but her praises seemed hollow and shallow. Still she persisted in getting up at six every morning to spend an hour in praise. She read psalms of praise and sang hymns of praise until feelings of praise began to fill her heart.

One morning she wrote, "I feel a flutter in my spirit, Lord!" A few days later she was able to say, "I am feeling Your presence again after so many months of darkness."

Not long after that, she penned, "A feeling rises up inside me that little trickles of praise are now running together, merging, beginning to form a small river of praise. It began mechanically, yet now has increasingly the feel of spontaneous emotion."

The power of praise had lifted Catherine Marshall out of the valley of despair and brought her into the very presence of Jesus. She found God again when she followed the admonition of Philippians 4:4 and began to "Rejoice in the Lord."

Epilogue

Following that experience Catherine wrote eight books, including: *Something More, Meeting God at Every Turn, Julie,* and *A Closer Walk*. Her son Peter and his wife were given two healthy children that brought joy to her heart.

Catherine is best remembered for her biography of her first husband, Peter Marshall, *A Man Called Peter*, which was on the *New York Times* bestseller list for more than fifty consecutive weeks. Her book, *Christy,* based on the life of her mother, sold more than 8 million copies.

With her second husband, Leonard LeSourd, an editor, she helped found a publishing company and a group called The Intercessors, which is a prayer fellowship, each member covenanting to pray for others.

1 Thessalonians 5:18

Give thanks in all circumstances,
for this is God's will for you in Christ Jesus.

Praise the Lord Anyhow!

Seventeen-year-old Joni Eareckson lay in the hospital on a strycker frame unable to move her body from the neck down. As the truth dawned upon her that she would be a quadriplegic for life as the result of a diving accident, she became depressed, resentful, and angry.

How could a good God permit something as terrible as this to happen to me when I was trying to live for Him, Joni wondered. She gave up on prayer and decided she wanted to die. She asked her friends to bring her medicine to help her die, but they refused. Then she felt more helpless than ever, since she could not even take her own life.

During those months of frustration a friend, Steve Estes, often spent time with her. He'd bring her pizza or donuts and read to her from the Bible. Joni listened because she liked his company, but she wasn't much interested in the words he read.

One day he read 1 Thessalonians 5:18, "Give thanks in all circumstances."

He closed his Bible and said, "Well, Joni, don't you think it's about time you got around to thanking God for that wheelchair of yours?"

"No way!" Joni responded. "I'm not thankful, and I won't say it. I won't give thanks when I don't feel like it."

"Whoa!" Steve replied. "Look at that verse again. It doesn't say that you have to *feel* thankful. It says to give thanks in all circumstances, good and bad, whether you feel like it or not."

"But how can I thank God when I can't understand why all this has happened to me?" Joni whined.

"We'll never understand the ways of God," Steve went on. "You don't need to know why; you need to be thankful that God is in your life, leading and helping you."

So Joni gritted her teeth and through her tears prayed, "OK, Lord, I thank You for this hospital bed. I would really rather have pizza, but if You want me to have cafeteria oatmeal, that's fine. And Lord, I thank You that physical therapy is helping me. Lord, I'm grateful that when I practiced writing the alphabet today with that pencil between my teeth it didn't look like chicken scratches."

It didn't happen overnight, but eventually Joni changed. She writes: "Thankful feelings began to well up. It was as though God rewarded me with the feeling of gratitude for having obeyed and given thanks."

Epilogue

Joni Eareckson Tada is an accomplished artist, speaker, and best-selling author in spite of her handicap as a quadriplegic. She is the director of JAF Ministries, an organization that brings together disabled people and the church through evangelism, encouragement, inspiration, and practical service.

She has written more than eighteen books. Some well-known titles are: *Joni, A Step Further, When Is It Right to Die, Diamonds in the Dust,* and *A Quiet Place in a Crazy World.*

Joni lives with her husband, Ken, a high school teacher, in southern California.

Hebrews 10:17

And their sins and iniquities
will I remember no more.

The Revolution That Failed

Maria was a rebellious teenager, a member of a large family of wealth and influence in Ecuador. In her rebellion, she ran away from a religious school. Her parents were firm with her. She had to choose. Either she returned to the convent school or she could no longer be considered their daughter. She said Goodbye to her family and left.

The Communists saw an opportunity to advance their cause. They befriended Maria and took her in. Within a few short years, she married three times and divorced three times. She gave birth to two children. Maria became a party leader and organized student demonstrations.

Then her mother died. The woman was of such stature that the bishop himself came to officiate at the funeral. Maria was there, but she mocked the bishop openly and ridiculed all he did. She made fun of him while her mother lay in her casket.

Pangs of conscience struck her even as she was mocking, but she thought it was nothing. However, in the months after the funeral, remorseful thoughts kept coming back to her. *How could she sink so low as to make a fool of herself at her mother's funeral? How could she be that disrespectful of her mother?* Somehow in her heart she felt it was wrong. Feelings of guilt swept over her. At night when she could not sleep she was filled with remorse for how she had disrespected her mother, the church, and God. Then she told herself, *But you don't even believe there is a God. Why do you feel like this?*

Her feelings of guilt so troubled her that she decided she must talk to someone. She made an appointment with Evangelist Luis Palau. When she came to see him, she had two football-player-sized bodyguards with her. She suspiciously looked around his office for listening bugs to see if her conversation would be recorded and the party betrayed.

Maria smoked cigarettes fiercely, lighting the next with the stub of the last. When she spoke, her voice dripped with poison and hatred. "You pastors and priests are a bunch of thieves and liars and crooks. All you want is to deceive people. All you want is money!"

She continued like that for twenty minutes, swearing, accusing, criticizing, and insulting. When she paused, Palau said, "Is there anything I can do for you? How can I help you?"

Maria took her cigarette from her mouth, stared at him for a moment, and suddenly began to sob uncontrollably. When she regained control, she said in a friendlier tone, "You know in thirty-eight years of my life, you are the first person who ever asked me if he could help me. All my life people have asked me for my help."

Palau asked her what her name was. Although she was suspicious, she agreed to tell him her name. "My name is Maria Benitez-Perez. I am the female secretary of the Communist party of Ecuador. I am a Marxist-Leninist. I am a materialist. I don't believe in God."

She then began another tirade of insults against preachers, priests, and the church. For three hours she shared the details of her life story and the report of her behavior at her mother's funeral. Finally she said, "Supposing there is a God, and I'm not saying there is, because I don't believe there is a God. But just supposing there is. If there is a God, which there isn't, do you think He would receive a woman like me?"

Palau opened his Bible to Hebrews 10:17 and turned it to her to read.

"But I don't believe in the Bible," she responded.

"You've already told me that," the pastor said. "But we're just supposing there is a God, right? Let's just suppose this is His Word. He says, 'Their sins and iniquities will I remember no more.'"

"But listen," she said. "I've been an adulteress, married three times, and in bed with a lot of different men."

He repeated, "Their sins and iniquities will I remember no more."

"But I haven't told you half my story. I stabbed a comrade who later committed suicide."

"Their sins and iniquities will I remember no more."

"I've led student riots where people were killed."

"Their sins and iniquities will I remember no more."

She continued to confess her sins, and seventeen times he repeated that verse. Finally she was silent. Then she spoke softly. "If He could forgive me and change me, it would be the greatest miracle in the world. He can't do it."

"Would you like to try it?"

"It would be a miracle."

"Invite Him into your life and try it. See what will happen."

After a long pause she said, "All right," and bowed her head. Palau led her into a prayer of acceptance, asking forgiveness and receiving Jesus into her life. By then she was crying.

A week later she came to see him again and told him she was reading the Bible and felt much better.

Epilogue

The next year Palau met her again. He was shocked. She looked happy, but her face was covered with purple bruises. Several of her teeth were missing.

She shared the story. She had told her comrades of her new faith. At a meeting of party leaders, she said, "I am no longer an atheist. I have become a Christian. I'm resigning from the party. We're all a bunch of liars. We deceive people when we tell them there is no God."

They tried to silence her, but there was a division, some demanding she be allowed to speak, others shouting her down.

A few days later, four of her comrades attacked her and smashed her face against a metal electrical box, leaving her for dead. After that, a missionary lady had studied the Bible with her.

That June, the revolution she had planned took place. Students and agitators made a disturbance in the streets of the capital. The army was called out. They planned to attack the army and overthrow the ruling military junta. The Communist leader was to come out of hiding in neighboring Colombia and take over the government.

On the morning of the revolution, the leader came out of hiding. He asked to see his long-time friend, Maria. He asked her, "Why did you become a Christian?"

"Come with me to the countryside, and I'll explain everything," Maria offered. "I'll show you what I've learned from the Bible." He agreed.

The disturbances that were to lead a revolution fizzled and died. Their leader was in the countryside studying the Bible with Maria.

Hebrews 13:8

Jesus Christ the same yesterday,
and today, and for ever.

Yesterday, Today, and Forever

Lunch was over, the dishes done, and Rita Armstrong stood a moment at the sink wondering what to do next. Her husband wouldn't return for several hours, and she could think of no urgent chores. *I've got the whole afternoon to myself,* she mused, feeling a rare sense of well-being and peace. *I think I'll just relax and spend a few moments with God.*

Making herself comfortable in her favorite chair, Rita leaned her head back and thought of the long years that had led to this moment. Since her teenage years, Rita had lived on an emotional roller coaster, spending weeks and sometimes months in the darkest depression, only to come out of it into an emotional high when she talked too much, drove too fast, and spent money like water. A doctor had finally diagnosed her as manic-depressive and had put her on a medication. Through the years she had often cried out to God, but He had seemed so far away, distant, uncaring.

Rita closed her eyes, and her thoughts traveled back in time to her traumatic childhood during the air raids in England in World War

II and the beginning of her emotional problems. *Where were You, God, in those dark times?* She scanned the centuries back to creation to a time when there was only God. Then she thought about the future, about the coming of Christ, and the end of all things. God would still be there.

She remembered the night at an evangelistic rally when she had gone forward to the altar to give her heart to Jesus. She remembered the sudden realization she had experienced that Jesus loved her enough to die for her. Her heart had gone out in love to Him, and she had known without a doubt that He loved her and accepted her.

Like a sudden flash of light, the words of Scripture came to her: "Jesus Christ the same yesterday, and today, and for ever."

Jesus cannot change! Rita thought. *He loved me when I was a child, He will love me when I get to heaven, and He loves me now!*

Joy and love overwhelmed her. Suddenly she realized she was significant in His eyes—that she mattered to Him! Jumping to her feet, Rita began to dance around the house singing over and over, "I matter to God! I matter to God!"

Reflecting back to that day, Rita declares, "After that experience my mood swings gradually stabilized and I began to feel a different person. Today I feel accepted and whole."

Epilogue

Eight years later, Rita's twenty-three-year-old son died of leukemia, but through it she was able to praise God for His love and care. Today she holds support groups for other Christians suffering from depression. She and her pastor husband continue to minister in various towns in England.

Revelation 3:4

Thou hast a few names even in Sardis which have not defiled their garments; and they shall walk with me in white: for they are worthy.

Thrown Out of Her House

Twenty-two-year-old Mary Bosanquet faced a major crisis in her young life. Mary's ancestors were French Huguenots who fled to England to escape religious persecution in France. Their descendants had prospered, and Mary's father was a wealthy and influential London merchant. The family belonged to "society." Her father was well-connected, knew all the "right" people. His daughter was provided the finest and most expensive clothing and jewelry.

But a gospel bombshell exploded in the Bosanquet mansion. Friends invited Mary to attend the meetings of John Wesley's "Methodist" society. She went without telling her father. And wealthy Mary Bosanquet was converted. She rejoiced in the personal assurance of forgiveness and salvation. She felt as though she were floating on clouds. She shared this happiness with her father. He was ashamed!

She invited her brothers to the Methodist meetings and spoke to them about their personal salvation. She began to dress plainly like the Methodists!

Her father confronted her and demanded, "Mary, I require you to make a promise to me."

"What is it, Father?"

"It is that you will never, now or in the future, try to make your brothers what you call 'Christians.' "

"Father, I dare not consent to that."

"Then, if you refuse to consent, you force me to put you out of my house."

Mary replied, "According to your view of things, I do."

Her father scolded, "You don't appreciate what I provide for you. You wear the plain clothes of 'those people.' "

Mary respectfully answered her father, "If I but think on the word holiness, or the adorable name of Jesus, my heart seems to take fire in an instant, and my desires are more fixed on God than before. As I cannot go with you anymore to places of amusement, so neither can I wear the expensive clothes you buy me anymore. I must be God's and His alone."

Her father asked her to pack her things. As she left his presence to pack her belongings in one simple trunk, she wondered what her future would be and how she would survive as an unmarried young woman. The promise of Revelation 3:4 came clearly to her mind: "And they shall walk with me in white: for they are worthy." She took courage that if God walked with her, she need not fear.

Her father called the family coach and sent her away. He did allow her young maid who was also a believer to go with her. From the manorial suburbs of the wealthy with their gardens and servants, her father's coach drove her to the poorhouses of Laytenstone.

Mary's new home had two rooms with a view of chimneystacks and the filthy yards of her poor neighbors. She began to "exhort" her neighbors and expound the Scriptures. Revival soon occurred, and a Methodist society was formed there.

Later she and her companions were given a farm in Yorkshire where she developed an orphanage for children.

Epilogue

Twenty years after she was sent from her father's home, she married John Fletcher, a prominent Wesleyan preacher who was also an Anglican pastor in Madeley, Shropshire. They pursued a joint ministry, with Fletcher preaching in the local church and his wife speaking regularly in the tithe barn. When her husband died, she carried on the parish ministry alone, with appreciation from the people.

Nine years after Mary's death in 1815, a hymn writer and poet, Henry F. Lyte, heard her story and inspired by it, wrote the well-known hymn:

> Jesus, I my cross have taken,
> All to leave and follow Thee;
> All things else I have forsaken,
> Thou from hence my all shall be.
> *SDA Hymnal,* No. 525.

Revelation 19:6

**And I heard as it were the voice of a great multitude,
and as the voice of many waters,
and as the voice of mighty thunderings,
saying, Alleluia: for the Lord God omnipotent reigneth.**

Saved From Financial Ruin

George Frideric Handel was a child musical prodigy. By the age of nine, he was writing spiritual cantatas. At ten he composed a set of sonatas. But his surgeon father insisted that he could not make a living composing music. He required that his son study law.

Despite his father's reluctance, George learned to play the organ and the violin, and at eleven he composed music for an entire church service each week. The royal court in Berlin heard of his amazing musical gifts and invited him to play before the future king of Germany.

Prince Earnest Augustus offered to send him to Italy to study music at the court's expense. But Handel's father refused to let him go. He asked him to come home and study law.

In his terrible disappointment, George read his Bible for encouragement. He read the passage in Ephesians 6:1 telling children to obey their parents in the Lord. He knew what he had to do. He informed the palace that he would obey his father and go home.

When he arrived home to enroll in the Lutheran Gymnasium in

preparation for law studies, he found his father in poor health. Every day after school, Handel hurried to his elderly father's room to read to him from the Bible. His father's favorite passages were the scenes of Jesus' birth, ministry, and death.

Then one evening quite by accident, the twelve-year-old boy turned to Revelation 19:6. Thinking his father might enjoy that passage, he read, "And I heard as it were the voice of a great multitude, and as the voice of many waters, and as the voice of mighty thunderings, saying Alleluia: for the Lord God omnipotent reigneth."

"Son, read that last sentence again," said his father with intense feeling. "And read it slowly."

"The . . . Lord . . . God . . . omnipotent . . . reigneth."

"Now read it again," said the old man, his eyes glowing.

George read those words to his father five times before the man was satisfied. That cold February in 1697, Handel's father died at seventy-five.

Handel became a much-appreciated musician in Germany. In 1713 when he was twenty-eight, George Frideric Handel moved to London. He found the aristocracy of England hungry for Italian opera. He wrote forty such works. But the taste of the fickle crowd changed. They no longer attended his operas, and Handel went heavily into debt and came to the verge of bankruptcy.

The London press began to ridicule him as a has-been. Unable to pay his bills, he suffered a stroke that paralyzed his right arm. Returning to Germany, he took water treatments and recovered the use of his hand. He returned to London only to be threatened by his creditors that he would be sent to debtor's prison if he did not pay his bills.

It was then that someone brought him a libretto with the title "Messiah." But instead of using just the gospels, the author employed the Old Testament prophecies of the coming of Christ as well. He used passages from many books of the Bible. He especially liked the passage from Revelation 19:6: "Alleluia: for the Lord God omnipotent reigneth." He remembered how he had read that verse to his dying father, and his father had asked him to read it again slowly.

On Saturday, August 22, 1741, Handel sat down at his desk in his London home and wrote on a blank music sheet the word *Messiah*. He bowed his head and asked God to bless him. Within minutes, the music began to leap from his pen. For twenty-four days he hardly stopped to eat or sleep.

A servant came into the room as he was concluding the "Hallelujah Chorus" and saw tears dripping on Handel's desk. The near-bankrupt composer exclaimed, "I thought I saw all heaven open before me and the great God Himself."

He performed it first in Dublin, Ireland. It was a great success. The news quickly spread to London. Handel was popular. His oratorios drew large crowds. He paid his debts.

When the *Messiah* was produced in London at Covent Garden, King George II was in the royal box. On the third hallelujah, the king stood and continued to stand throughout the chorus. Since the king stood, the entire audience rose to their feet. Handel watched as chills ran up and down his spine. He was blinded by his own tears. God had used him. The oratorio had accomplished its purpose. The king of England publicly honored the King of kings.

Epilogue

Handel continued to compose great religiously themed oratorios. They had titles such as *Saul, Joshua, Solomon*, and *Joseph and His Brethren*.

He began an annual concert featuring the *Messiah* to benefit a home for orphans, the Foundling Hospital.

Handel died in 1759 at the age of 74. He lies buried in Westminster Abbey in London. The *Messiah* lives on!

eople Index

References

Introduction
Christianson, Evelyn. *What Happens When God Answers.*

Exodus 20:2: Touched at Her Bedside
Boreham, F. W. *Life Verses,* Grand Rapids, Mich.: Kregel Publications, 1994, 2:57-61, 67.
Douglas, J. D., and Philip W. Comfort, eds. *Who's Who in Christian History.* Wheaton, Ill.: Tyndale House Publishers, Inc., 1992, 237.
Encyclopedia Britannica. Chicago: William Benton, Publisher, 1965, 361, 362.
Lewis, D. M., ed. *Dictionary of Evangelical Biography,* Oxford, UK: Blackwell Publishers Ltd., 1995, 1:361, 362.
Moyer, E. S., ed. *The Wycliffe Evangelical Dictionary of the Church.* Chicago: Moody Press, 1982, 134.

Exodus 20:3-5: Conflict in Korea
Spangler, Ann, and Charles Turner. *Heroes.* Ann Arbor, Mich.: Serv-

ant Publications, 1990, 333-356.

Turner, Charles. *Chosen Vessels*. Ann Arbor, Mich.: Servant Publications, 1985, 159-183.

Esther 4:16: Sawdust Surrender

Mayer, E. S. *The Wycliff Biographical Dictionary of the Church*. Chicago: Moody Press, 1982, 431.

White, Ellen G. *Life Sketches*. Nampa, Idaho: Pacific Press® Publishing Association, 1943, 20-24.

White, Arthur L. *Ellen G. White: The Early Years*. Hagerstown, Md.: Review and Herald Publishing Association, 1985, 36, 37.

Psalm 11:1, 3: Singing on the Scaffold

Douglas, J. D., and P. W. Comfort, eds. *Who's Who in Christian History*. Wheaton, Ill.: Tyndale House Publishers, 1992, 460.

Durant, Will, and Ariel Durant. *The Age of Reason Begins*. New York: Simon and Schuster, 1961, 124-130.

Encyclopedia Britannica. Chicago: William Benton, Publisher, 1965, 14;994-997.

Seventh-day Adventist Bible Commentary Hagerstown, Md.: Review and Herald Publishing Assoc., 1954, 13:657.

Psalm 23: Island Hiding Place

Boreham, F. W. *Life Verses*. Grand Rapids: Kregel Publications, 1994, 5:210.

Encyclopedia Britannica Chicago: William Benton, Publisher, 1965, 8:817; 9:793-796; 16:11-13; 19:779; 20:266; 23:593, 594.

The World Book Encyclopedia. Chicago: Field Enterprises Educational Corporation, 1973, 21:251.

Psalm 32:1: A Poet Finds the Secret

Lewis, D. M. *Dictionary of Evangelical Biography*. Oxford, UK: Blackwell Publishers, 1995, 2:1169-1171.

Douglas, J. D., and P. W. Comfort, eds. *Who's Who in Christian His-*

tory, Wheaton, Ill.: Tyndale House Publishers, 1992, 708, 709.

Encyclopedia Britannica. Chicago: William Benton, Publisher, 1965, 23:515.

Pollock, John. *John Wesley.* Wheaton, Ill.: Harold Shaw Publishers, 1995, 93-100.

Psalm 37:3: Career Crisis

Gordon, Anna A. *Frances E. Willard.* Chicago: The L. W. Walter Company, Publishers, 1898, 92-105.

Hammack, Mary L. *A Dictionary of Women in Church History.* Chicago: Moody Bible Institute, 1984, 158.

Moyer, Elgin S. *The Wycliffe Biographical Dictionary of the Church.* Chicago: Moody Press, 1982, 435.

Tucker, Ruth A., and Walter Liefeld. *Daughters of the Church.* Grand Rapids: Zondervan Books, 1987, 271-274.

Psalm 81:10: Faith to Feed Thousands

Lewis, D. M. *Dictionary of Evangelical Biography.* Oxford, UK: Blackwell Publishers, 1995, 2:803, 804.

Douglas, J. D., and P. W. Comfort, eds. *Who's Who in Christian History.* Wheaton, Ill.: Tyndale House Publishers, 1992, 494.

Mayer, Elgin S. *The Wycliffe Biographical Dictionary of the Church.* Chicago: Moody Press, 1982, 288.

Pierson, A. T. *George Mueller of Bristol.* London: Pickering & Inglis, Ltd., 1972.

Watts, Dorothy Eaton. *This Is the Day.* Hagerstown, Md.: Review and Herald Publishing Association, 1982, 347.

Psalm 91:11: Facing Death at Sea

Douglas, J. D., and P. W. Comfort, eds. *Who's Who in Christian History.* Wheaton, Ill.: Tyndale House Publishers, 1992, 483-485.

Encyclopedia Americana. Danbury, Conn.: Grolier Inc., 1990, 19:428.

Harrell, Irene Burk. *God Ventures.* Waco: Word Books, 1970, 41-45.

Mayer, Elgin S. *The Wycliffe Biographical Dictionary of the Church.*

Chicago: Moody Press, 1982, 281-282.

Pollock, John. *A Fistful of Heroes*. Basingstoke, Hants, UK: Marshall, Morgan, and Scott Publications, Ltd., 1988, 112-118.

Pollock, John. *Moody: The Biography*. Chicago: Moody Press, 1983, 297-307.

Woodbridge, John, ed. *More Than Conquerors*. Chicago: Moody Bible Institute, 1992, 140-147.

Psalm 107:43: Floating Treasure

Lewis, D. M. *Dictionary of Evangelical Biography*. Oxford, UK: Blackwell Publishers, 1995, 1:328, 329.

Douglas, J. D., and P. W. Comfort, eds. *Who's Who in Christian History*. Wheaton, Ill.: Tyndale House Publishers, 1992, 214.

Encyclopedia Britannica. Chicago: William Benton, Publisher, 1965, 7:738.

Lockyer, Herbert Sr. *Psalms, A Devotional Commentary*. Grand Rapids: Kregel Publications, 1993, 430, 437.

Mayer, Elgin S. *The Wycliffe Biographical Dictionary of the Church*. Chicago: Moody Press, 1982, 124.

Watts, Dorothy Eaton. *Steppingstones*. Hagerstown, Md.: Review and Herald Publishing Association, 1987, 359.

Psalm 118:17: The Battle for the Bible

d'Aubigne, J. H. Merle. *The Reformation in England*. Carlisle, Penn.: The Banner of Truth Trust, 1985, 1:79-100.

Douglas, J. D., and Philip W. Comfort, eds. *Who's Who in Christian History*. Wheaton, Ill.: Tyndale House Publishers, Inc., 1992, 735.

Lockyer, Herbert Sr. *Psalms, A Devotional Commentary*. Grand Rapids: Kregel Publications, 1993, 526, 527.

Mayer, Elgin S. *The Wycliffe Biographical Dictionary of the Church*. Chicago: Moody Press, 1982, 441, 442.

Tuttle, Mark, ed. *Christian History,* no. 2. Worcester, Penn.: Christian History Institute, 1983, 2:2-5, 10-30.

References

Psalm 121:1, 2: Hiking at Gunpoint

Dortzbach, Karl, and Debbie Dortzbach. *Kidnapped.* New York: Harper and Row, Publishers, 1975.

Watts, Dorothy Eaton. *Never Thirst Again.* Hagerstown: Review and Herald Publishing Association, 1996, 113, 114.

Psalm 133:1: Seven Survivors

The Encyclopedia Americana. Danbury, Conn.: Grolier Incorporated, 1990, 13:443.

Lackyer, Herbert Sr. *Psalms, A Devotional Commentary.* Grand Rapids: Kregel Publications, 1993, 685.

Psalm 139:9, 10: Whaleboat Rescue

Boreham, F. W. *Life Verses.* Grand Rapids: Kregel Publications, 1994, 33-43.

Lansing, Alfred. "Endurance." *Great Lives, Great Deeds.* London: The Reader's Digest Association, 1965, 245-263.

Paddock, C. L. *Highways to Happiness.* Washington, D.C.: Review and Herald Publishing Association, 1950, 32, 33.

Encyclopedia Britannica. Chicago: William Benton, Publisher, 1965, 20:432.

Proverbs 3:5, 6: Facing Bankruptcy

Flood, Robert G. *On the Waters of the World.* Chicago: Moody Press, 1989.

Isaiah 26:3: Shalom! Shalom!

Encyclopedia Britannica. Chicago: Encyclopedia Britannica, Inc., 1965, 11:131. Gariepy, Henry. *Songs in the Night.* Grand Rapids: William B. Eerdmans Publishing Company, 1996, 11, 12. Hooper, Wayne, and Edward E. White. *Companion to the SDA Hymnal.* Hagerstown, Md: Review and Herald Publishing Association, 1988, 459, 460.

Osbeck, Kenneth W. *101 Hymn Stories.* Grand Rapids: Kregel Publications, 1982, 206, 207.

Osbeck, Kenneth W. *52 Hymn Stories Dramatized.* Grand Rapids: Kregel Publications, 1992, 124-126.

McCutchan, Robert Guy. *Our Hymnody.* New York: The Methodist Book Concern, 1937, 374.

Sheppard, W. J. Limmer. *Great Hymns and Their Stories.* Fort Washington, Penn.: Christian Literature Crusade, 1979, 27-29.

Isaiah 43:2: Out of the Ashes

Snowflakes in September. Nashville: Dimensions for Living, 1992, 83.

Isaiah 6l:1-3: Courage in a Prison Camp

Rose, Darlene Deibler. *Evidence Not Seen.* San Francisco: HarperCollins, 1990, 109-113, 223, 224.

Watts, Dorothy Eaton. *Never Thirst Again.* Hagerstown, Md.: Review and Herald Publishing Association, 1996, 56, 57.

Ezekiel 33:8: Before the Thunderbolt

Dick, Lois. "Summoned by the Thunderbolt," *Signs of the Times,* December 1988.

Douglas, J. D., and Philip W. Comfort, eds. *Who's Who in Christian History.* Wheaton, Ill.: Tyndale House Publishers, Inc., 1992, 123.

Tucker, Ruth A. *Guardians of the Great Commission.* Grand Rapids: Zondervan Publishing House, 1988, 85-88, 129, 130.

Watts, Dorothy Eaton. *Never Thirst Again.* Hagerstown, Md.: Review and Herald Publishing Association, 1996, 83, 84.

Habakkuk 3:17, 18: Through Plague and Fire

Boreham, F. W. *Life Verses.* Grand Rapids: Kregel Publications, 1994, 2:137-148.

Castleden, Rodney. *British History.* London: Parragon Book Service, Ltd., 1994, 134, 135.

Encyclopedia Britannica. Chicago: William Benton, 1965, 14:272; 17:990.

References

Zechariah 3:2: The Runaway Shoemaker

Boreham, F.W. *Life Verses.* Grand Rapids: Kregel Publications, 1994, 2:87, 88.

Lewis, Donald M. *Dictionary of Evangelical Biography.* Oxford, England: Blackwell Publishers, Ltd., 1995, 843.

Hooper, Wayne, and E. E. White. *Companion to the Seventh-day Adventist Hymnal.* Hagerstown, Md.: Review and Herald Publishing Association, 1988, 56, 57.

McCutcheon, Robert G. *Our Hymnody.* New York: The Methodist Book Concern, 1937, 26, 27.

Matthew 6:14, 15: The Guard's Impossible Request

Marshall, Catherine. *Adventures in Prayer.* Old Tappan, N.J.: Fleming H. Revell Company, 1975, 94, 95.

ten Boom, Corrie. *The Hiding Place.* New York: Bantam Books, 1971, 237-239.

Tucker, Ruth, and Walter Liefeld. *Daughters of the Church.* Grand Rapids, Mich.: Zondervan Publishing House, 1987, 395, 396.

Watts, Dorothy Eaton. *Friends for Keeps.* Hagerstown, Md.: Review and Herald Publishing Association, 1995, 150.

Woodbridge, John. *More Than Conquerors.* Chicago: Moody Press, 1992, 84-89.

Matthew 6:33: The Empty Wallet

Douglas, J. D., and Philip W. Comfort, eds. *Who's Who in Christian History.* Wheaton, Ill.: Tyndale House Publishers, Inc., 457.

Marshall, Catherine. *Mr. Jones, Meet the Master.* London: Collins Fontana Books, 1954.

Marshall, Catherine. *A Man Called Peter.* New York: Avon Books, 1951, 15-45.

Moyer, Elgin S. *The Wycliffe Biographical Dictionary of the Church,* Chicago: Moody Press, 1982, 264.

Watts, Dorothy. *This Is the Day.* Hagerstown, Md.: Review and Herald Publishing Association, 1982, 103.

Matthew 18:14: Flames, Fear, and Faith
The Best Stories From Guidepost. Wheaton, Ill.: Tyndale House Publishers, 1987, 35-38.

Matthew 11:35: A Veteran's Victory
Fisk, Samuel. *More Fascinating Conversion Stories.* Grand Rapids: Kregel Publications, 1994, 35-40.
Moyer, E. J., eds. *The Wycliffe Biographical Dictionary of the Church.* Chicago: Moody Press, 1982, 77, 78.

Matthew 27:32: The Man They Didn't Want
Boreham, F.W. *Life Verses.* Grand Rapids, Mich.: Kregel Publications, 1994, 3:234, 235.
Douglas, J. D., and Philip W. Comfort, eds. *Who's Who in Christian History.* Wheaton, Ill.: Tyndale House Publishers, Inc., 1992, 625.
Encyclopedia Britannica. Chicago: William Benton, Publisher, 1965, 20:693.
Warren, Max. *Simeon.* Church Book Room Press Ltd., 5-23.

Matthew 28:20: Facing Death in the South Seas
Boreham, F. W. *Life Verses.* Grand Rapids: Kregel Publications, 1994, 3:128-139.
Douglas, J. D., and Philip W. Comfort, eds. *Who's Who in Christian History.* Wheaton, Ill.: Tyndale House Publishers, Inc., 1992, 532.
Howell, Clifford G. *The Advance Guard of Missions.* Nampa, Idaho: Pacific Press® Publishing Association, 1912, 258-286.
Lewis, Donald M. ed. *Dictionary of Evangelical Biography.* Cambridge, Mass.: Blackwell Publishers, Ltd., 1995, 2:858.
Moyer, Elgin S. *The Wycliffe Biographical Dictionary of the Church.* Chicago: Moody Press, 1982, 317.
Paton, James. *The Story of John G. Paton.* New York: A. L. Burt Company, Publishers, 1892, 182-187.

John 6:37: A Book Born in a Crisis

Arnott, Anne. *Valiant for Truth.* Grand Rapids: Wm. B. Eerdmans Publishing Co., 1985.

Boreham, F. W. *Life Verses,* Grand Rapids: Kregel Publications, 1994, 1:62-72.

Bunyan, John. *Grace Abounding to the Chief of Sinners.* Springdale, Penn.: Whitaker House, 1993.

Douglas, J. D., and Philip W. Comfort, eds. *Who's Who in Christian History.* Wheaton, Ill.: Tyndale House Publishers, Inc., 1992, 117, 118.

Fisk, Samuel. *40 Fascinating Conversion Stories.* Grand Rapids: Kregel Publications, 1993, 2-30.

Harrison, Frank Mott. *John Bunyan.* Carlisle, Penn.: The Banner of Truth Trust, 1964.

Kerr, Hugh T., and John M. Mulder, eds. *Famous Conversions.* Grand Rapids: Wm. B. Eerdmans Publishing Company, 1983, 48-53.

Moyer, Elgin S. *The Wycliffe Biographical Dictionary of the Church.* Chicago: Moody Press, 1982, 67.

Fisk, Samuel. *40 Fascinating Conversion Stories.* Grand Rapids: Kregel Publications, 1993, 27-30.

Harrison, Frank Mott. *John Bunyan.* Carlisle, Penn.: The Banner of Truth Trust, 1964.

Kerr, Hugh T. and John M. Mulder, eds. *Famous Conversions* Grand Rapids: Wm. B. Eerdmans Publishing Company, 1983, 48-53.

Moyer, Elgin S. *The Wycliffe Biographical Dictionary of the Church.* Chicago: Moody Press, 1982, 67.

Rupp, Gordon. *Six Makers of English Religion: 1500–1700.* Plainview, N.Y.: Books for Libraries Press, 1957, 92-101.

Woodbridge, John D. *Great Leaders of the Christian Church.* Chicago: Moody Press, 1988, 265-270.

Romans 3:24, 25: Coping With Mental Illness

Adams, Robert M. *The Land and Literature of England.* New York: W. W. Norton and Company, 1983, 335, 336.

Boreham, F. W. *Life Verses.* Grand Rapids: Kregel Publications, 1994, 1:120-128.

Douglas, J. D., and Philip W. Comfort, eds. *Who's Who in Christian History.* Wheaton, Ill.: Tyndale House Publishers, Inc., 1992, 177, 178.

Durant, Will, and Ariel Durant. *Rousseau and Revolution.* New York: Simon and Schuster, 1967, 810-813.

Osbeck, K. W. *101 Hymn Stories.* Grand Rapids: Kregel Publications, 1982, 264, 265.

Romans 6:23: Salvation in One Minute

Blanchard, Ken. *We Are the Beloved.* Grand Rapids: Zondervan Publishing House, 1994, 15-36.

Romans 8:28: The Longest Weekend

Bright, Vonette Zachary, ed. *The Greatest Lesson I've Ever Learned.* Milton Keynes, England: Nelson Word Ltd., 1993, 44-49.

Christenson, Evelyn. *What Happens When God Answers.* Dallas: Word Publishing, 1986.

Christenson, Evelyn. *Gaining Through Losing.* Wheaton, Ill.: Victor Books, 1984.

Watts, Dorothy Eaton. *Never Thirst Again.* Hagerstown, Md.: Review and Herald Publishing Association, 1996, 48.

Romans 8:31-39: Dearer to Her Than Life

Barstad, Glenna. *They Dared for God.* Nampa, Idaho: Pacific Press® Publishing Association, 1958, 80-84.

Encyclopedia Britannica. Chicago: William Benton, Publisher, 1965, 6:676; 20:154, 155.

Watts, Dorothy Eaton. *Never Thirst Again.* Hagerstown, Md.: Review and Herald Publishing Association, 1996, 124.

1 Corinthians 10:13: He Could Not Call God A Liar

Graham, Franklin. *Rebel With a Cause.* Nashville: Thomas Nelson,

Inc., 1995, 125-129.

Watts, Dorothy Eaton. *When Your Child Turns From God*. Hagerstown, Md.: Review and Herald Publishing Association, 1997, 17, 18.

2 Corinthians 12:9: A Washerwoman's Faith

Deen, Edith. *Great Women of the Christian Faith*. San Francisco: Harper San Francisco, 1955, 233-237.

Hammack, Mary L. *A Dictionary of Women in Church History*. Chicago: Moody Press, 1984, 135.

Smith, Amanda. *An Autobiography: The Story of the Lord's Dealings With Amanda Smith*. London: Hodder and Stoughton, 1894.

Tucker, Ruth A. and Walter Liefeld. *Daughters of the Church*. Grand Rapids: Zondervan, 1987, 270, 271.

Watts, Dorothy Eaton. *The Best You Can Be*. Hagerstown, Md.: Review and Herald Publishing Association, 1993, 11-13.

Woodbridge, John D., ed. *Ambassadors for Christ*. Chicago: Moody Press, 1994, 60-63.

Philippians 4:4: Light in Her Darkest Night

Beeson, Ray, and Ranelda Mack Hunsicker. *The Hidden Price of Greatness*. Wheaton, Ill.: Tyndale House Publishers, 1991, 169-177.

Hammack, Mary L. *A Dictionary of Women in Church History*. Chicago: The Moody Bible Institute, 1984, 98, 99.

Marshall, Catherine. *Something More*. New York: McGraw-Hill, 1974, 1-18, 44-51, 133-136.

Marshall, Catherine. *Light in My Darkest Night*. New York: Avon Books, 1990.

Tucker, Ruth A. *First Ladies of the Parish*. Grand Rapids: Academie Books, Zondervan, 1987, 236-242.

1 Thessalonians 5:18: Praise the Lord Anyhow!

Tada, Joni Eareckson. *Joni*. Grand Rapids: Zondervan Publishing House, 1976.

Tada, Joni Eareckson. *A Quiet Place in a Crazy World*. Sisters, Ore.:

Multnomah Books, 1993, 147-149.
Watts, Dorothy Eaton. *Friends for Keeps*. Hagerstown, Md.: Review and Herald Publishing Association, 1995, 203.

Hebrews 10:17: The Revolution That Failed
Palau, Luis. *Calling the Nations to Christ*. Chicago: Moody Press, 1983, 11-21.

Hebrews 13:8: Yesterday, Today, and Forever
Howat, Irene. *Light in the Middle of the Tunnel*. Fern, Ross-shire, Scotland: Christian Focus Publications, 1994, 8, 109-122.
Watts, Dorothy Eaton. *Never Thirst Again*. Hagerstown, Md.: Review and Herald Publishing Association, 1996, 45.

Revelation 3:4: Thrown Out of Her House
Konkel, W. *Living Hymn Stories*. Minneapolis: Bethany House, 1982, 33-39.
Lewis, Donald M.,ed. *Dictionary of Evangelical Biography*. Cambridge, Mass.: Blackwell Publishers, Ltd., 1995, 1:394.

Revelation 19:6: Saved From Financial Ruin
Douglas, J. D., and Philip W. Comfort, eds. *Who's Who in Christian History*. Wheaton, Ill.: Tyndale House Publishers, Inc., 1992, 301, 302.
Ludwing, Charles. *George Frideric Handel*. Milford, Mich.: Mott Media, 1987, 1-179.
Moyer, Elgin S. *The Wycliffe Biographical Dictionary of the Church*. Chicago: Moody Press, 1982, 181, 182.